Dancin' With Shirley

By Alan Liere

Also by Alan Liere

Bear Heads and Fish Tales
. . . and pandemonium rained

Dancin' With Shirley

By Alan Liere

Cover Design and Illustration
  By Mark Stenersen

Page Layout and Typography
  By Charles B. Summers
  Pacific Publication Services
  P. O. Box H
  South Bend, WA 98586

Publisher
  Pease Mountain Publications
  P.O. Box 216
  Deer Park, WA 99006
  Fax: 509-276-2707

Dancin' With Shirley

Copyright ©1999 by Alan Liere.

All rights reserved. No part of this book may be reproduced in any manner without the express written consent of the author, except for brief excerpts in critical reviews and articles

For information or orders contact:
Pease Mountain Publications
P.O. Box 216
Deer Park, WA 99006
Fax: 509-276-2707

Library of Congress Cataloging in Publication Data:
Liere, Alan W., 1944-
    Dancin' With Shirley

1. Hunting—Anecdotes, facetiae, satire
2. Fishing—Anecdotes, facetiae, satire

ISBN: 9652697-1-x
LCCN: 98-91278
Printed in United States of America

Dedication

For Marie (Lacey) Liere, the prettiest girl at the dance.

Pease Mountain PUBLICATIONS

P.O. Box 216 Deer Park, Wa. 99006

Table of Contents

Author's Note	10
A Lingering Regret	11
I Never Wanted a Pony	14
The Other Man	17
Hawking	21
Snakes Are Good For You	24
Dear Sid	29
The Lease	32
Swimming with the Manatees	36
How To Get Rich Crappie Fishing	39
The Primordial Man	45
Sneak 707	48
Gun Walkin'	53
The Christmas Teal	56
Dear Mrs. Scrimshaw	61
Another Expensive Lesson	64
The Spot	67
Heroes	71
Dancin' With Shirley	74
The 'Gar	80
Lots of Something	83

Dear Steve 86
I'll Just Sit Here and Read 89
The Dog, Walter! 92
Eatin' Dust 95
This Kid 98
The Curse 104
And Here's Another Tip. 107
Dear President Clinton 110
The Ultimate Snipe Hunt 113
I'm Not Tired, I'm Happy 117
OH, Canada! 120
Shortcuts Ain't 123
The Pffftt-Click Season 127
Bullhead Saturday 130
A Sign For Pease Mountain 134
Until I Married Lacey 137
Dear Donald 140
Just Like In The Movies 143
Christmas Eve Day 148
Those Birds In Thurmond's Garage 151
I'd Rather Be A Codger Than A Crank 156
Grandpa's False Teeth 159
Inland Tuna 163
Dear Dr. McNumnenson 166
The Bomb 169
Lumbago, She Says 173
Evolution Of A Hunter 176
Bird Brains 181
Lacey's Featherbed 184

A Matter Of Adaptability 187
A Sigh For March 190
Dear Burt 192
The Most Obliging Critter I Know 195
Cleaning The Creek 200
Marty 203
About the Author 206
To order additional copies of this book: 207

Author's Note

    Ever since I became old enough to notice there are people who *don't* fish and hunt and generally recreate in the outdoors, I have felt obligated to attempt to explain to them why I *do*. My passions, it seems are not as enthusiastically embraced by everyone, and there are even those who are intolerant of the way I am.

    The way I see it, the outdoor life is the only *real* life there is, and the question is not "Why do I fish and hunt?" but rather "Why doesn't everyone?" I suppose I could enjoy some of Mother Nature's delights by merely *being there* on a warm Snake River sand bar or high above the rim rock in Wawawai Canyon. I guess I could drive 60 miles to sit in a boat down where the wild inlet stream boils into Rock Lake, or perhaps stretch out on a mud flat beside Seven-Mile Slough with no purpose other than to observe. Without a fishing rod, a rifle, or a shotgun, though, I'd feel like part of me was missing.

    Life is a dance delightfully complicated by diverse tastes, opposite opinions, and screen doors that unexpectedly slam shut. You can fall on your face at a dance, but you can also fall in love. In this collection of short stories, it's obvious I've done both.

Alan Liere
Loon Lake, Washington

A Lingering Regret

I have made a fair number of poor choices in my life, but with only a few of them has the regret lingered much beyond a month or so. The day I stuffed my father's favorite pipe with caps was one of those times. When Dad finally checked out of the hospital (minus his eyebrows), he made certain I spent the rest of a very long, very hot summer on my knees at the end of a pair of hand-operated grass clippers.

This year, just three days before Lacey's birthday, I made another poor choice that has had lingering ramifications: I ordered my wife a robe from one of those stylish women's lingerie catalogs because they promised delivery in 24 hours, and frankly, I was desperate. You know how it is, I'm sure—you've already decided what it is you want for that special someone, and because it is so unique and you know right where to find it, you do not worry about whether it will be there even if you have waited too long to pick it up. Then, you go in to get it and it is GONE.

Now, Lacey has always been pretty easy to buy for, but three days before a birthday is not conducive to conscientious shopping. To compound my distress, it was right in the middle of the pheasant season and my vehicle had developed a clunk in the transmission that suggested my mechanic was about to become very happy. It was easy enough to get friends to take me hunting, but I hated to ask them to take me shopping, too.

On the verge of a full-blown panic, I happened across the lingerie catalog my Aunt Judy had left on the floor by the big easy chair on her last visit. I do not normally peruse lingerie catalogs, of course, and until my aunt forgot hers, I did not even know there were companies that specialized in garments made with less than a square foot of material. And though I love outdoor catalogs, I could tell from the cover there weren't going to be any shotguns or clay pigeon throwers in the one Aunt Judy left behind. I opened it with the same sense of guilt I used to feel when I snuck a look at my uncle's *Playboy.*

It took quite a bit of looking, but lo and behold, amid the scalloped underwire bras with Venice lace detailing, and the bathing suits cut clear to **there**, I eventually located and ordered a tasteful "azalea-coloured" robe that wouldn't show off my wife's navel. This was important because, though those magazine models seemed mighty proud of their belly buttons, my wife despises hers. Lacey thinks belly buttons should be illegal and females who *intentionally* show them should be put in homes for the tacky. I tend to agree.

The robe arrived, as promised, in time for her birthday, and Lacey liked it just fine. The problem is, since that day, we have received an average of two lingerie catalogs pe*r week* from the same company, and one per lifetime is plenty. I see no substantial difference in their pre-spring, early-spring, pre-summer, late summer, and late, late summer catalogs.

Unless this glossy paper avalanche stops soon, there will be no room left in the garage to park my duck boat or the tent trailer. I'm certainly no tree-hugger, but I do hate to see forests leveled just so the women's lingerie catalog people can keep filling my mailbox with promotional text that overuses the words "sweet, chic, sexy, fun, charge card," and "$49.95."

It is not likely I will ever again order an "azalea-coloured" robe, and, frankly, I don't know anyone who would be willing to even try on some of that other stuff. The women for whom I buy gifts have normal legs that look good in canvas brush pants, and they aren't likely to "slip on a more beautiful body for summer" because they can't afford cosmetic surgery. Their legs start at the bottom with well-callused feet and get proportionately larger as they go up. They do not stand half-naked on stick legs on their verandas with one hip in the air, staring at other half-naked women.

Still, the folks in the lingerie business keep stuffing the mailbox with the fashion industry's equivalent of drivel. And the really neat thing is, *all of these catalogs have my name on them!* Try explaining that to your mailman. Try explaining that to your kids. In glowing terms, they advertise "romantic favourites" that can "defy nature, turn back time, and give you back your natural lift." Their products come in an assortment of "colours" like kiwi, tangerine, and azure. There's not a red, yellow or camouflage brown in the bunch.

I just can't relate to a catalog that can't spell "color," doesn't carry shotguns, and doesn't have a single item in camo. If anyone out there is having a paper drive, I'd appreciate a call.

I Never Wanted a Pony

When I was a kid, my friends and I spent a lot of time playing with plastic cowboys and Indians and horses. I think plastic had just been invented; they were making *everything* out of it, and I thought it was about the coolest thing since red wax Halloween lips.

Ronnie Zink lived across the vacant lot from me. He was three years older, also appreciated plastic, and had an uncle with a horse ranch near Clayton, Washington. Because of this kinship, Ronnie claimed to know everything there was to know about pintos and mustangs and scallions and nightmares. He taught me a lot of relatively obscure horse trivia, like why horses have yellow teeth (too many sugar cubes) and why they are shod with such odd-shaped metal shoes (perfect for making ringers). Ronnie also taught me how to make a distinctive "galloping" sound with my tongue when my plastic horse chased his across the back yard sidewalk which was really a salt flat in Utah. So unquestionable was Ronnie's expertise in these horse affairs, he even claimed the right to name the plastic replicas we played with. His was "Silver" of Lone Ranger fame. Mine was "Gelding" of no fame whatsoever. "It's a really cool name," he told me seriously. "A lot cooler than 'Silver'." I believed him, and for the rest of the summer, the alley behind my house was daily witness to the thunder of hooves, a cloud of dust, and a mighty "Hi-ho Gelding—away!"

Oddly enough, the desire to own a *real* pony was never much of a childhood consideration. I didn't even ask. In the first place, I figured parents who wouldn't let me have a dog "because they make such terrible messes" would never agree to staking out a Trigger Jr. in the back yard and letting him have his way with the azaleas. Early-on, my pets were of a marine variety—guppies and goldfish and once in a while a wild and crazy snail.

In the second place, my Uncle Vern in Moses Lake owned a surly mule named Precious who chased me across a pasture the first time I tried to feed him carrots. Then he tried to eat my black low-cuts as I struggled through the rail fence. And while it is true Precious was not a horse, I had noted a strong resemblance. I wanted nothing to do with even a distant relation to an animal that preferred Converse tennis shoes over carrots.

My next encounter with a live horse-like animal occurred three years later at Camp Reed on Fan Lake. During "free time" we "campers" were offered a variety of activities which included turtle races, leather crafts, canoeing, and horseback riding. What I actually wanted to do was race turtles. I figured I could beat a turtle, but my cousin and fellow camper, Steve Hailey, dared me to go on a trail ride with him instead.

My camp "driver's test" consisted of correctly answering the question, "Have you ever been on a horse?" I said "yes," but didn't mention the fact it had been a wooden Appaloosa from the merry-go-round at Natatorium Park.

What Precious had not entirely accomplished, 'Ol Rennie did. 'Ol Rennie knew the faster he made the four-mile loop around the lake, the sooner he would get back to his oats. We began our jaunt with the instructor in the lead and 'Ol Rennie and I bringing up the rear. In 12 seconds, however, 'Ol Rennie had accelerated from 0 to 60, passing everyone in sight. In four minutes, we had gone around the lake and were back at camp. During the entire "ride," my seat did not once come in contact with the saddle. When we got back to the barn, the Pend Oreille County volunteer fire department was pulling in, having mistaken my terrified, airborne shrieks for a call to action.

My distrust of horses was now complete, and for several decades I managed to avoid them entirely. Then, I was married, the father of many, and the proud but somewhat financially embarrassed owner of 22 country acres. In this setting, Katie, the youngest daughter, turned on me. The other kids had been content to merely *read* books like *Black Beauty*, *King of the Wind*, and *Old Bones the Wonder Horse*; Katie, however, wanted a pony! "Why?" I questioned her. "We have chicken and beef in the freezer."

Twelve-year-old Katie fixed me with a disgusted look. "It has been proven," she said, "that horse ownership instills responsibility, discipline, and self-esteem. And besides that," she added, "it prolongs the likelihood of girl-boy interaction well past puberty, and if you go halvsies with me I'll clean your truck."

And that's why Fanny, a huge, Thoroughbred mare came to live with us. And that's also why young, competent Dr. Koesel of the Deer Park Veterinary Clinic recently left our place with a check which pretty much wiped out the entertainment budget for the year. It's also why I have reoccurring muscle spasms in my lower back. Holding the head of a Thoroughbred mare that objects to having a tube threaded through her nose into her esophagus can be traumatic to all concerned. Except to Katie. Katie, of course, wasn't home. Sixteen-year-old Katie was out somewhere not interacting with a boyfriend.

The Other Man

When I first met Mike on a spring rafting trip, I would never have suspected he could cause a marital rift. Oh sure, Lacey and I had the usual spats, but nothing some of my creative groveling wouldn't eventually resolve. I had sometimes teased that the only thing she liked to make for dinner was reservations, and she always countered by suggesting restaurant lobster was less expensive than the occasional pheasant or trout I brought home. Mostly, though, ours was a sound relationship based on concessions to one-another's eccentricities. No way could another man interrupt our lives.

Until I met Mike, the only thing that stood between me and a whole houseful of mounted game birds were things Lacey deemed important—little things like food, clothes, and furniture. Granted, we had a small house. Granted, I already had a mounted pheasant, a mounted chukar, and a mounted mallard. But those were mere token tributes to my passion for bird hunting. I dreamed of whole flocks of mounted partridge and bluebill and sage hens and quail. I wanted them skulking across my book shelf, preening on the end table, flying out of the wall above the fireplace. How I mourned the many fine specimens I had baked and stuffed in my mouth because Lacey said we had neither the room nor the money to do otherwise.

As luck would have it, Mike was not only the perfect hunting partner, he was also a talented taxidermist. We took our first outing together in late October, returning to the car on a golden autumn morning with nine California quail. "These are really fine specimens," Mike said, as we laid them out to admire. "Would you like me to mount a pair for you?"

"That'll be the day," I lamented. "If I bring home any more mounts, Lacey will have me looking for my shoes under the bed of some shoddy motel."

"I can do them in just a few hours," Mike persisted. "I'd really like to mount a pair for you."

"Can't do it," I said reluctantly. "Lacey would have a fit."

"I'll even put them in a habitat scene," Mike said.

"Doesn't matter," I insisted. "Lacey was very emphatic."

"Won't cost you a dime," Mike said.

"Okay."

Mike put the quail on an oak base complete with artificial snow and resin icicles dripping coldly from a sprig of wild rose. Even Lacey was beguiled the day I brought them home.

"You're sure they didn't cost you anything?" she said, hiding her enthusiasm with a yawn.

"I knew you'd be ecstatic, dear," I gushed. "Observe the realism, the intricate attention to detail. Notice how the subservient female stares lovingly into the eyes of the male."

"Observe the clinging dust," Lacey said. "See the artificial snow being ground into my carpet. And she's not being subservient, she's wondering why he's such a dork."

After accepting that first gift from Mike, it became all too easy to widen my eyes with pleasure and shake my head "yes" when he offered to do other mounts. To compound the temptation, we were hunting together constantly. A Hungarian patridge in an autumn habitat scene was a mounted memory of a November foray into Whitman County. After that came a majestic snow goose in full flight and a pair of ruffed grouse—all without charge, all without Lacey's blessings. And I couldn't say "no." The following October, Mike gave me a mourning dove and a band-tailed pigeon, but it wasn't until he delivered the Merriam's gobbler that Lacey really put her foot down.

"No!" she said, stomping my instep. "I will not have that buzzard look-alike leering at me while I'm eating. Absolutely, positively, NO!"

"It didn't cost anything, dear," I pleaded, using the justification that had worked so well before. "We could put it in the bedroom."

"No. I don't care. It's ugly. It's neck looks like someone dribbled candle wax down a feather duster."

"Those are the wattles, Precious," I explained. "Mike did a masterful job."

Lacey examined the fowl again, just to make sure she hadn't missed anything. "I won't have it in this house," she said.

The following days were marked by an uneasy truce. The mounted gobbler still stood tentatively near the double doors in the dining room and Lacey went about the house humming as she is inclined to do when she has decided to never again speak to me. Judiciously, I honored this request for silence by quietly reloading shotgun shells in the shed. When she served cold tofu casserole the third night in a row, I knew this standoff would last longer than most, but I didn't really comprehend the scope of her anger until I returned from work one night and noticed a stranger sitting in my easy chair reading my newspaper.

I found Lacey in the kitchen. "I notice there's a strange man sitting in my easy chair," I said, the first words between us in four days. "He's got the sports page laying all over the place. You know how I hate that."

Lacey looked up from the cold casserole she had taken from the refrigerator. She was still humming. "He's not so strange," she said. "A little young, perhaps, but not strange. His name is Felix. Isn't he handsome?" The humming again.

"Is this Felix someone I need to know?" I asked, scowling. "He appears to be making himself quite at home."

"You and your birds are out of here," Lacey said abruptly, ignoring my question. "Felix is a really nice guy. He'll be staying."

"Listen, Lacey," I hissed, "I'm not sure what is going on, but I don't like it. If you think I'm going to sit back and have some strange man eating *my* tofu casserole at *my* table, you've got another think coming."

"Don't be ridiculous," Lacey said. "I wouldn't make Felix eat this stuff. We'll barbecue him a steak. It's in my best interests if he keeps up his stamina."

"Lacey! Lacey. . . ."

Don't worry about it," she said. "You'll hardly see him. We'll be most active while you're at work."

"But Lacey. . . . What will the neighbors say? What about the kids?" I couldn't believe it had come to this.

"The kids can help," she said. "They won't be in the way. I'm sure they'll learn something. It will be educational."

"H-h-help!" I groaned. "Help?" I was sputtering badly, part numb and partly outraged. "It'll be a cold day in . . . ."

"Now calm down," Lacey said, patting me on the back. "This little affair won't last forever." She smiled sweetly. "And this way you can keep that old turkey and I'll never have to look at it."

"Turkey?" I mumbled. "Is that what caused this? Right now, I don't give a . . . ."

Lacey cut me off again. "As soon as Felix finishes the framing, he and I can do the paneling and then I'll lay the carpet. When we're both finished, you can fill the new room to the rafters with your mounted birds." She smiled again. "Durwood next door assured me Felix is an excellent carpenter. He needed a place to stay until his wedding next month, and I thought. . . ." Lacey cocked her head and gave me a funny look. "Are you all right, dear?" she asked. "Felix said it wouldn't cost very. . . ."

"Lacey?" I interrupted.

"Yes?"

"Are we really having tofu casserole again tonight?"

Lacey looked down at the quivering mass she had liberated from the refrigerator. "Do you have a better idea?" she asked.

"I've got this extraordinary urge to pay too much for dinner," I said. "Why don't you make reservations for 7:30 at The Ivy?"

"I already have," Lacey smiled. "For 6:30. Go change."

Never have I put on a tie with more smugness. A den of my very own! It's amazing, I thought, what I can accomplish when Lacey puts her mind to it.

Hawking

A couple Saturdays ago, I was able to do something I have always wanted to do. No, you are wrong about that. I have never cared one whit about touching my nose with my tongue. That is my brother-in-law, Thayer the Abnormal you are thinking of. What I have always wanted to do (besides not work for a living) is go hawking.

Those of you not familiar with hawking need to know right now it is not the process of coughing up and spitting out the lining of your esophagus. There is a name for that, but I'm sure it is spelled differently. The "hawking" to which I refer is the one known as "The sport of kings." You do it with raptors, which are birds with beaks and talons that can put a good-sized dent in your nose if you put it up real close to them and wiggle it like a bunny. The peregrine falcon is probably the best known hawking bird, but Harris, Cooper, and red-tailed hawks are probably more commonly used here in these parts.

After several months of trying to finagle an invitation from the Washington Falconers Association to attend a meet, I was finally invited to the Tri-Cities where several members of the organization would gather for the final hunt of the season.

On Saturday, a friend, Jay Cummins, and I accompanied Danny Pike and Jerry Fraulini into the sage brush country outside of Richland. At least it *used* to be outside of Richland. Urban sprawl is gobbling up the open spaces at an alarming rate, and what had just three years previously been an uninterrupted expanse of sweet-smelling sage, was now a 50-acre patch lined on two sides by houses, swimming pools, and fenced back yards with yappy dogs. When Danny and Jerry freed their Harris hawks to hunt, in fact, the first thing the birds did was sail to the roof top of the closest house and perch there like fierce-looking weather vanes checking out the local canine population.

In but a few seconds, we had kicked up a jack rabbit, and both birds accelerated from their vantage points, skimming the sage tops, relentlessly pulled toward their fleeing quarry. Immediately, Danny, Jerry, and Jay, were off at a dead run, yelling "Flight! Flight! Flight!" and making noises that sounded like a cross between an ambulance siren and a coon dog. Its primordial origins startled me, and before I could consider my tender Achilles and sore hamstring, I was off like a jet. Well—a locomotive anyway. . . Okay, an 18-wheeler. . . An 18-wheeler with flat tires.

The rabbit escaped, but its route had taken it along a wooden fence and across the yard of a lady who had been washing her Pontiac in the driveway. From two sides of her corner lot, asphalt wound deep into the neighborhood where hundreds of houses that had displaced acres of sagebrush were arranged tastefully 10 feet apart on lanes, avenues, and cul-de-sacs with cutesy names like Sagewood, Sandysage, and Sageview.

In horror, the lady dropped her garden hose, aghast at the natural spectacle that had just unfolded. She was red-faced, nearly bubbling with outrage. "You guys are despicable!" she called when we stopped in the field next to her to get our breath.

Danny and Jerry ignored the tirade. Obviously, they'd heard it before. But this was new to me, and I turned in confusion to face the lady with the red face. "Are you talking to us, ma'am?" I asked politely.

"Despicable!" she fumed again, and I couldn't help but smile as I envisaged Daffy Duck saying the same thing and spitting all over himself as he violently lisped the word.

"Killing innocent bunnies!" She went on. "Low-lifes! Assassins!" She turned and stomped from the cement pad, onto her cement porch, and into her four-bedroom frame house with wall-to-wall carpet and an indoor jacuzzi. Once inside, she glared at us through the window, across her quarter-acre manicured lawn where jack rabbits had once browsed and meadow larks had once nested.

And I was thinking about the hundreds of bunnies that no longer had a place to live in the sagebrush just outside Richland, Washington.

Snakes Are Good For You

As a youngster, I appreciated nothing better than the adrenalin rush of being scared to within inches of death. Sometimes, this could be accomplished in my feeble-minded but optimistic efforts to take a go-cart of my own design down the Division Street Hill, and sometimes it was as simple as a forbidden, starlit, nightcrawler safari into the yard of our eccentric and somewhat psychotic neighbor, "Gravel" Gertie Bone. Neither of these endeavors, however, could hold a candle to the lingering horror generated by settling deep into a musty sleeping bag on my grandmother's screened back porch and letting the white-haired lady scare me with stories about snakes.

Grandma Burress had grown up on a farm in Missouri's Ozarks where she personally encountered hoop snakes that could take their tails in their mouths and roll after a child faster than he could run. There were glass snakes, too—vicious, fragile creatures that would break into a hundred pieces if you messed with them, each piece instantly becoming another venomous threat. Snakes that plotted revenge, snakes that lay in ambush, and snakes that made themselves flat and slid under your bedroom door—Grandma Burress knew them all. It was no wonder that long after she had left the screened porch and gone inside, I would lie there alone, listening for dry-slithery sounds in the flower beds and imagining all sorts of terrible, death-dealing serpents.

Oddly enough, while Grandma's snake stories scared me, the snakes themselves did not, and as I was growing up, I not only accepted their presence, I was fascinated by it. Still, it was not until a few summers ago that I realized how useful snakes had been in my life. It was a late August afternoon when my brother-in-law, Thayer the Abnormal, spotted me as I and a nice stringer of bluegill emerged from Hailey's Glade, a tired woodlot nearly within the city limits. Thayer had been trying for years to find the secret source of my outsized bluegills, and when I saw him driving by, I ducked down in the weeds and cursed the fates that had brought us together only a hundred yards from the flooded gravel pit.

"I see-e-e you," Thayer called when he had slammed to a stop. "So that's where yer honey hole's at! Woulda never thought to look so close to home." Already, he was pulling a rod and tackle box from the back seat. "Heck, I didn't even know there was water back there," he said, getting out of the car. "Very good, brother-in-law, ver-ry good indeed."

"Ahhh—Thayer," I began, "it's a real small pond. I'd appreciate it if you would keep it . . . "

"Can't wait to bring the boys," Thayer gushed.

. . . to yourself," I finished lamely. For some reason, Thayer was never happy fishing unless surrounded by his friends from the unemployment line, and I knew the two-acre pond could not stand the pounding they would give it.

Grinning obliviously, Thayer hiked up his trousers and brushed by me mumbling. "Got just the thing," he was saying as he disappeared into the trees. "Gonna catch every. . . ."

"Watch out for snakes," I said quietly.

There was a silence of perhaps ten seconds, and I knew Thayer had stopped walking. Then, several twigs cracked sharply and his head reappeared above a red dogwood, the eyes rather pleasantly fearful, the mouth pursed tightly but twitching just a little. "Snnnnaakkes?" he said, the word rising in tone as he forced it from his chest.

"Western diamondbacks," I offered. "The usual. There's lots of 'em." I leaned back against Thayer's car and chewed nonchalantly at a thumb nail, feeling very fine. It really didn't matter if my pond was guarded by venomous pit vipers or harmless bullsnakes, and it didn't matter, either, how many there were. For Thayer, *one* snake, any variety, was too many.

Thayer sort of pirouetted out from behind the dogwood and tip-toed quickly back towards me, much like a person trying to navigate a meadow muffin-mined pasture while being intimidated by a snorting bull. "That was a mean thing to tell me, brother-in-law," he said angrily. "That was pure-dee-spiteful!" He made one final, rather graceless leap, grabbing for the car door in mid-air and flinging himself inside, huffing. "You probably ain't never seen a single snake all the time you been comin' here."

"So why aren't you fishing, then?" I asked.

"Because you mighta," he whined. Thayer threw his rod into the back seat and slid over behind the wheel. With an offended glare, he drove off. I almost felt sorry for him. Unfounded though it was, his fear was genuine.

Interesting, I thought. Very interesting. In the years since my grandmother had passed on, I had never really considered the value of snakes beyond their one-time worth as antagonists in some delightful stories. Obviously, this misunderstood, limbless vertebrate had other uses also. To verify this hypothesis, I went home and filleted bluegill, then sat down with a pencil and paper and began to reminisce. An hour later, I had composed this five-point list under the penetrating heading:

Why Snakes Are Good

1. Snakes Make You Laugh.

Personally, I am most fond of a laugh that progresses to the point of discomfort, one that explodes violently and increases in velocity by the second. A gut-busting "can't get my breath" roar that brings tears to my eyes and concerned stares from others in the vicinity—that is the kind of laugh I appreciate. I have experienced this exquisite pain only a few times, the most memorable taking place last summer on a camping trip: my friend, Mike Sweeney, found two road-killed rattlesnakes one evening—just little fellows. He secretly placed them in a brown paper sack and the next morning, he extended the sack graciously to Eddie, another friend. "Want a piece of pepperoni?" he asked. When Eddie reached in and withdrew one of the headless inhabitants, his "Yeee-owwl!" cracked windows 80 miles away and put the Air Force Reserves on weekend alert. Mike and I laughed so hard we cried.

2. Snakes Make You Healthy.

A good snake scare will flush ugly cholesterol from the arteries more effectively than a five-mile sprint. It will bring the heart to maximum working capacity in half the time it takes to put on an aerobics tape. My friend, Eddie, (See #1) is a case in point. Before the "pepperoni" incident, Eddie was a walking heart attack. Now, however, he is 20 pounds lighter, having burned off much of the excess as he re-entered the atmosphere.

3. Snakes Save You Money.

This spring, my wife's cousin, Birdy, came to visit. For several years, Birdy has been on a diet, eating and drinking only food items that begin with the letter "A"—like "A" chocolate cake, "A" pound of bacon, "A" side of beef, "A" box of donuts, "A" case of beer, etc. After three days with us, it was obvious we could not afford to feed her, and when she was in an eating frenzy, I was afraid to leave her alone with the dog. On the fourth evening, I casually asked Birdy if she had yet been visited by the big gopher snake that lived under the guest room floor. The next morning at breakfast, Birdy had large, black bags under her eyes, said she'd had trouble sleeping, and asked if we would mind terribly if she went home to her own bed.

4. Snakes Make Diplomacy Possible.

Though he's not a bad guy himself, my wife's Uncle Lem has the worst bird dog in creation. Badger bullies younger dogs, hunts on the fringes of infinity, and thinks the estrus is an on-going phenomenon. After our initial chukar chase together, I vowed I would never again accompany Lem and Badger afield. "Lem," I said, "you're taking a mighty big chance with Badger on these chukar hunts. Why, those canyons are just crawling with rattlers."

"But we need a dog," said Lem, who is not particularly afraid of snakes himself. "What'll we do?"

"Tell ya what, partner," I said. "Let's just use my Lab. Shoot, I could replace that worthless old hide in a minute, but a fine animal like Badger, etc., etc."

5. Snakes Can Make You a Legend.

Though my grown children have considerately not made me a grandfather, I have become a friend, a teacher, and a hero to the children of a dozen acquaintances—a legend, if you will. Why? Well, I read a whole bunch, and I remember a lot of what I have read about snakes. I know that poisonous snakes have bifid tongues that carry odors to the roofs of their mouths for examination. I know their fangs are hollow, fold up when not in use, and are periodically shed. I know the venom is hemotoxic, the rattles are composed of the same material as human fingernails, and that the eggs are incubated and hatched within the female. More importantly, though, I have seen an eight-foot eastern diamondback grab his tail and turn himself inside out. I have seen a southern copperhead steal milk from the udder of a Holstein heifer, and I know a place where wonderful, weird hoop snakes chase little boys and girls down dark alleys.

The kids are scared spitless. Grandma Burress would be tickled.

From the Desk of
Alan Liere

Dear Sid:

Good to hear from you again. Seems like ages since we plowed through snow drifts to get to that pheasant draw behind Miller's barn. I know you New York boys have some nasty weather of your own, but I promise, those were truly unusual conditions for early December in these parts, and I hope you were able to save at least some of your nose. Nasty stuff, that frostbite.

Should you decide to risk another trip to Loon Lake during bird season, you might want to invest in a ski mask. Don't do like my cousin, Dooley, though, and wear it into a bank. Dooley isn't up for parole until 2008. He probably shouldn't have carried his shotgun in with him. Said he didn't want to leave it in the car because the doors didn't lock.

Steve Heath, the fellow who took you duck hunting the day I had to work, sends his best and says he'll have a real retriever the next time you come over. He apologizes again for making you do all the water work. Steve bought a chocolate Lab in March, and it should know at least as much as he does by November. He calls it Freud. Currently, he is in the process of teaching Freud to fetch pheasants, but in my estimation, it's taking much longer than necessary. Having been a psychologist so long, I think Steve forgets the dog is not paying him by the hour. He spends a lot of time just "counseling" poor Freud. The last time I was over there, Steve was trying to convince the mutt that while chewing the leg off the piano was "socially unacceptable behavior, it didn't make him a bad dog." He told me he thought Freud's "obstreperous comportment could be modified by expatiating the positive denouements of being the ninth pup of an eight-nipple bitch." On second thought, Sid, maybe you'd better just work on your side stroke if you plan on hunting with Steve again. You might want to pick up a wet suit, too.

Fishing has slowed down some here on the lake, what with the water skiers and all. The town kids were out last weekend for their annual mid-summer wingding, and I swear the swim-wear manufacturers must be making a killing on women's bathing apparel. I haven't seen a suit yet with more than five square inches of material. Some of those gals had legs that appeared to go all the way to their arm pits, and though I did appreciate the scenery, I forgot why.

You'll never believe it, Sid! When I got home from work last Friday, there were four honest-to-goodness wild Merriam's gobblers in the big bull pine in the front yard. I chased those silly-looking fowl all over the county this last spring and didn't drop a feather, and then there they sat as sassy as you please by my front window. The neighbors were all gathered in the street gawking and taking pictures, and it was all a lot of fun until someone decided to call Turkey John.

When John shows up in full camouflage, the situation deteriorated badly. Now, here's a man I've never even met, but he sets up a turkey decoy in my petunias, puts a diaphram call in his mouth, squats down behind my pickup with a 10-gauge, and starts clucking. Before long, he's got the turkeys gobbling, the dogs barking, and everyone getting kind of nervous. John, it seems, has been chasing turkeys without success for 11 years, and the accumulation of frustrations made his elevator stop between floors. He sat there a-cluckin' and a-smilin' until almost dark, and he was still smiling when Sheriff McDonald put him in the back seat and drove off. I doubt that much will come of it, however, as the shotgun wasn't even loaded and McDonald is a turkey-hunting fanatic himself.

I guess I told you when you were here that I was leaving in August for a caribou hunt in Alaska. Lacey keeps asking me why I want to hunt caribou, and to be honest, I don't know. Because I haven't done it, I guess—an excuse to drive 5,000 miles in my own good company. Seems like every day I find more white in this beard of mine, and I feel an almost desperate need to wring as much life as possible from my alotted years. Lacey says the savings account won't take much more wringing, but caribou steak makes a lot more sense to me than women's bathing suits. What do you think, Sid?

Keep in touch,

Alan

The Lease

In his book, *Studies in Pessimism*, printed in 1851, Arthur Schopenhauer says the two foes of human happiness are pain and boredom. In a storage shed my wife calls "That freakin' rat's nest," built in 1991, I smash my thumb with a framing hammer and decide Arthur Schopenhauer is right. It's the first week in January and I'm double-dipping my misery, bored to tears.

The duck season has ended. Pheasants, too. There's not enough ice on the lake to fish safely. Anything to do—anything at all—and I wouldn't be in a cold, confused, storage shed trying to put up a sheet of peg board my wife thinks will magically eliminate the clutter. Now I have a sore thumb too, and I've started to swear. I always start to swear when the forces of evil have defeated me.

What I really want to be doing is happily freezing to death in a goose blind. But the geese have been gone three weeks, destroying my late-season plans with a premature exodus. A goose-hunting man should not be compelled to compete with hammer and nail when he could be freezing to death with a shotgun and a retriever. I contemplate the hateful piece of pegboard again. My thumb nail, like my thoughts, is turning black.

Lacey slogs out to the rat's nest in her parka and stands unnoticed in the doorway with her arms folded and her laugh lines growing tighter. She eavesdrops as I speak bitterly to the hammer, then offers her message: "Phone," she says. "It's Mike."

The hammer clatters to the floor. Lacey jumps back and I rush through the door. "Are you expecting something?" she calls as I clear the snowy driveway and hit the porch running.

"Anything!" I yell back. "Anything."

Mike Sweeney is excited. He tells me the weatherman is calling for a week of warm winds—chinook winds we called them when we were kids and they came as surely as Santa Claus each winter. It's been many years since we've had a real chinook.

"Of course, that doesn't do us much good today," Mike admits, "but there might be some puddles in the scabrock by next weekend. The geese used to follow the winds back up. Want to give the old pond a look next Saturday?"

"Boy, you must be desperate," I tell him. "I went by there in October, looking for pheasants. It was dry as a bone and the guy's cows wrecked the blind."

"Well, do you?" Mike asks impatiently. "Ed does."

"Of course," I say. "What else is there?"

Six summers before, the three of us had optimistically taken a 10-year lease on the four-acre pond. Cheap. Too cheap—a hundred dollars a year. There had been great plans for our first lease.

We constructed a fine blind and made a list of rules for how often we would hunt it and on what days, and how we would handle guests. And then the pond dried up. No sense complaining to the rancher, though; the drought wasn't his fault, and he'd already spent the grand.

I pass another week in the storage shed without additional maiming, but Lacey suggests I schedule a personality transplant. I'm on edge. With something to look forward to, the days pass even more slowly. Outside, a warm wind blows seductively, melting the snow in the yard, washing miniature arroyos the length of the driveway. Maybe it is happening OUT THERE, too. OUT THERE where it really matters.

Friday night I dream fitfully. There IS water in the

scabrock. The geese HAVE followed the chinook wind north to the green winter wheat. They are feeding early and loafing away the afternoon. On the scabrock ponds. On MY scabrock pond. On The Lease. I'm already making coffee when the alarm I forgot to shut off awakens my wife.

Following a 45-minute drive, Ed, Mike, and I leave the pavement and follow a muddy, rutted path that parallels a weary fence line. Two miles east, then two miles north; we're getting close. Is that it off to the right? Is there water, or is the moon playing tricks on wet mud? I stop the truck in the darkness and Ed rolls down the window. "Damn!" he whispers. A reverent oath.

"What?" I ask.

"Turn it off," he says. "Shut off the engine."

I comply and lean over him toward the open window. The sky is clear and the air is still warm for January, and I can hear them honking nervously on the pond. I begin to shake. "What shall we do?" I whisper.

We decide on a frontal approach—go in, flush the birds in the dark, and set up. Hopefully, some will come back.

The pond is not deep, but the water has nearly filled out its contours. In the glimmering moonlight, it looks as it did six years earlier when we paid the grand.

Eddie makes a V in the shallow water with 15 shell decoys, and Mike and I wrap burlap camouflage netting around what remains of the blind. The cows have been thorough in their demolition. "Sixty yards to the last one," Eddie tells us, and we nod. Maybe it's good, maybe not. We have no idea what will work on this pond. Six years and we have no idea, so we cut long-stemmed wheat grass and weave it into the net because we have been successful on past hunts where we camouflaged our blind with long-stemmed wheat grass.

Darkness still. Low conversation. My black Lab, Dude, nudges me for a caress and hot coffee sloshes from a plastic mug and soaks through my coveralls. Eddie laughs, then spills his, too. Mike's survives until a lone "ha-ronk" directly over the blind sends us scrambling. Without circling, six honkers slide over the decoys and set down on the other side of the pond.

"Out of range," Eddie hisses mournfully.

"Too early, anyway," Mike replies.

For me, the shaking begins again. We take turns peeking at the birds over the top of the blind, but by dawn it is obvious they like it where they are. The smart thing would be to scare them off so others will not be tempted to the spot across the pond. We discuss this strategy in low voices, but there have been no others and we decide against it; it's fun to have them in sight.

The second flock comes in low and unannounced from the north, but Eddie spots them in time and Mike hits them with two seductive honks as they pass. They seem to swap ends in mid-flight and hustle back, dropping their large, black feet, their wings slowing their descent with a "whoosh, whoosh." One of my favorite sounds. "On the X, Sweetheart," Eddie is praying. "Put 'em on the X." I'm not sure who "Sweetheart" is, but the lead honker settles on Eddie's X in the middle of the V, 35 yards out.

"Take 'em!" someone yells. Later, Mike says it was I, but I do not remember. Eleven geese scramble for altitude and six splash back down. Dude tears away one side of the blind as he exits; I tear away the other. Mike and Eddie go over the top. We converge half way between the blind and water, shouting joyously, congratulating, forgiving previous debts and trespasses, cheering for the dog who already has one goose and seems relatively unaffected by the prospect of retrieving five more. Like small children returning from a holiday, we point and jabber and jostle, trying to reconstruct every detail of what we have done. I take pictures and we're still out of the blind when the next flock arrives.

No one seems to care except Dude, who stares from us to the departing flock, and back again. We all laugh as he stretches out in the sun and sighs deeply. Six years. Six Canadas. A great day in a bad month. February and March lurk ominously in the wings, but this memory will get us through.

Swimming with the Manatees

A couple years ago when Lacey and I were making plans to attend a national outdoor writers' conference in Haines City, Florida, we wrote to their Department of Tourism. Soon, they were filling our mailbox with literature about things to see and do while visiting the Carjack State. There were many interesting choices, ranging from Everglade tours and tarpon fishing to airboat rides and a mermaid show near Weeki Wachee Springs. The activity that really caught Lacey's eye, though, was swimming with the manatees. She was serious about it, and she thought I should be, too.

Until the literature from the Florida people, I thought manatees were a joke—something like The World Famous Alligator Boy I once saw in an Ilwaco, Washington museum. Come to find out, they were real—one of God's many attempts at humor. Also called sea cows, manatees are slow-moving, seal-shaped mammals with broad, shovel-like tails. Normally, an adult is 8-10 feet long, but some varieties attain lengths up to 14 feet.

There's no way I'm swimming with a manatee," I told my wife. "They're huge!"

"But they're docile," Lacey countered. "And so cute!"

"Rabbits are cute and docile," I said. "And they only weigh a few pounds. If you think we should swim with cute mammals, why not rabbits?"

Lacey grunted and gave me THAT LOOK—the one that makes me feel like I've been caught playing with my own brain in the bathtub.

"Well, how about muskrats?" I stammered. "I've swum with muskrats under the dock here in Loon Lake before. That's kind of fun."

"We human beings are so very arrogant," Lacey said. "I would think swimming with manatees would be a humbling experience. The purpose is to engage a large creature in its own environment."

"I've done that, too," I said. "In Benny Jefferson's hot tub. The large creature was Sarah Dinkleman. It was more scary than humbling, though."

"Spare me the details," Lacey said sarcastically. "I'm on my way to shop for a new bathing suit."

If you must know, the real reason I didn't want to swim with the manatees was that I didn't want to be seen in public with a 3,000 pound creature that looked better without a shirt than I did. When Lacey started talking about manatees, I began having this recurring dream in which a little boy saw me swimming and began to cry. "Will I look like that too, someday?" he blubbered to his father.

In another, similar dream, a little girl pointed at my pasty vastness as I bobbed among the manatees and said to her mother, "The white one isn't cute like the others, Mommy. What happened to the white one?" In my very worst nightmare, the little girl turned into my wife, Lacey, and ran away with Richard Simmons.

Alas, the adequate physique I maintained through my 30s and 40s, has deserted me during my 50s. The last couple years, the slow southern migration of flesh has become a mass exodus, and I know if it continues at its present rate, by the time I am 60, I will be able to tie my shoes, zip my pants, and put on my hat, all in the same motion.

I used to look forward to the new warmth of April so I could doff my shirt and begin my summer tan. The last few years, my idea of "getting some rays" has been to wear a short-sleeved shirt. Even my beloved cut-offs have been relegated to a bottom drawer in my dresser. My legs, which just yesterday were long and muscular are now just long. And white. Pasty, actually—like my fathers, who wouldn't have been caught dead in a bathing suit. "A workin' man doesn't have time for a suntan," he used to say.

Dad sure as heck wouldn't have gone swimming with a manatee.

Neither did I.

How To Get Rich Crappie Fishing

My wife said she was surprised we'd invited Richard to our neighborhood poker game a second time. "Isn't he the nice-looking single fellow who took all your money last month?" she asked. "The one you said could not come back until it snows in hell and the devil puts on a Santa suit?"

"That was Thayer that said that, not me," I corrected, jerking a thumb in the direction of my brother-in-law. "I merely remarked I thought it rude that a newcomer would walk in, get lucky a few times and then leave early just because he had to go to work."

"Yeah," Thayer grumbled. "He only stayed six hours."

"So why did you invite him back?" Lacey asked, using her foot to straighten the throw-rug between kitchen and living room. "It's obvious the man is an insensitive mercenary." She looked impishly from me to Thayer. "It's also obvious he plays poker better than you."

"The truth is, Lacey," I explained, "Richard just bought himself a new truck, and Thayer and I thought it would be neighborly if we helped him break it in."

Lacey's hands went to her hips. "Oh come on, you guys!" she said angrily. "You're not going to ask that perfectly nice young man to drive his new vehicle out to Cow Lake! You don't mean to tell me it's crappie season again!"

"It's crappie season again, dearest," I affirmed.

Lacey shook her head in disgust. "You've both ruined your vehicles on the road into Cow Lake. Now you want to ruin Richard's too?" She pointed an accusing finger at me. "There's still a clunk in the Pinto from last year," she continued, "and the mechanic said if the oil pan takes another shot like the last one, we can start buying 50-weight by the drum."

"But that's just the point, sweetheart," I cooed. "If we can get Richard to drive, we won't have those kinds of troubles. And too, his 4x4 has more clearance than the Pinto, and he won't have to gun it so hard to make it over Satan's Hump or across Ha-Ha Wash. Besides that," I said magnanimously, "Richard is new to this area and we want to start him out right."

Thayer had executed a cowardly, crab-like sidle when Lacey raised her voice, and he was reaching for the door knob when someone knocked on the other side. "It's Richard," he said, peeking out the peek hole.

Throwing up her hands in resignation, Lacey retired to the kitchen. "You guys show some compassion," she warned.

Richard Ainsworth was a likeable sort—15 years younger than I, but likeable still; there are just some things in a man one cannot intelligently begrudge.

"Now remember, Thayer," I whispered as he unlatched the door, "let's be subtle about this. We don't want Richard thinking we only invited him over so he would take us fishing. Play it cool and let me do the talking." I looked intently for a flicker of understanding. "Got it?"

"Got it," Thayer said.

I opened the door. "Hi, Richard," I gushed, laying a hand affectionately on his shoulder. "How'd you like to take us fishing?"

Thayer beamed. "In your new Bronco," he added. Despite the fact Thayer is not a blood relative, he has nevertheless been cursed with the family gene for impetuousness.

Richard grinned, looking from me to Thayer. "Before or after the poker game?" he asked .

"After, by all means," I said. "We don't even have to leave

until tomorrow morning." I then inaugurated an enthusiastic description of Cow Lake and its platter-sized crappie. I told how we had discovered it on a goose hunting expedition, and how the rancher and owner of the property, Sutton Grimes, had winched us out of Ha-Ha Wash. I related the fortunate circumstances that allowed us to return the favor a few weeks later when Mr. Grimes lost his driveline in front of the cafe where Thayer and I were eating lunch, and how we had run him and his daughter, Aurilla, around town looking for parts, and how Thayer had got them back on the road again. "But best of all," I said, "he told us that little lake was full of crappie, and if we were to close the gates, we could fish there anytime we wanted."

"I don't fish, fellas," Richard interrupted.

Now there was something for which I was unprepared. It had never ocurred to me that somewhere in the world existed a man who did not count fish slime and sunburn among life's pleasures. Richard's innocent disclosure left me speechless. Thayer, however, immediately grasped a thread of the delicate snarl and yanked.

"Ya drive, don'tcha?" he barked.

"What we're trying to do here, Richard," I soothed, attempting to unwrinkle our botched plans, "is include you in a little expedition we were planning for tomorrow. We realize you are new to this area, and thought perhaps you would enjoy joining us in a little piscatorial recreation."

"I thought we was going fishin'," Thayer complained.

Richard appeared undaunted by the exchange. "I tried fishing once but didn't care for it," he admitted. "My uncle took me with him for. . .for. . . ironheads, I think he called them. We didn't catch any."

"You mean *steelhead*," I corrected, "and it's no wonder you didn't catch any. The steelhead is a mythical fish, Richard. Your uncle was playing a joke on you—the fishing equivalent of a snipe hunt. But don't feel bad," I continued, "because Thayer and I pursued steelhead for years before we figured out they don't exist."

Thayer nodded. "That's right, son. But this is no steelhead chase we're planning for tomorrow; it's an honest-to-goodness fishing trip. If we get to Cow Lake, we'll catch crappie." Richard seemed unconvinced, but Thayer wasn't about to give up. "And you're just liable to get rich if you go with us tomorrow," he added.

I was about to come up with another plug of my own for Cow Lake when Thayer came up with that one, but I plopped down on the couch instead. It had been difficult enough trying to make a point with Thayer supposedly in my corner. Now, it seemed, he was pulling in a different direction, plumbing the depths of the ludicrous, and I knew all I could do was sit back and watch him give the family a bad name.

"Yup," Thayer continued, "we figured you could probably become a wealthy man in short order if you was to come crappie fishin' with us tomorrow."

Richard smiled condescendingly, but his eyes betrayed an interest. "Do tell me more," he said.

"Well, son," Thayer began, "as you may or may not know, in addition to some 40-odd square miles of range land, Cow Lake, and 10,000 head of beef, Sutton Grimes has a beautiful daughter."

"Is that right?"

"That's right, son," Thayer affirmed. "Isn't that right, brother-in-law?"

"Beauty is in the eye of the beholder," I said. Actually, Aurilla Grimes was not beautiful in the classic, modern, or contemporary sense of the word, but she did have some fine qualities. The best, of course, was her daddy's crappie lake.

"And," Thayer continued, "if I'm not mistaken, Sutton Grimes just recently said something about her finding a man so he'd have a son to take over the ranch."

"You're talking marriage?" Richard asked a little timorously.

"That's right, son," Thayer said, slapping him heartily on the back. "Congratulations. I know you and Aurilla will have a wonderful life together. And," he said, nudging Richard in the ribs, "it doesn't hurt to have a father-in-law with a couple million bucks, either."

"No. . . I suppose not," Richard said slowly, "but. . . but. . . it's all so sudden. Don't you think Aurilla and I should spend a little time together first—you know, sort of get acquainted?"

"Well certainly," Thayer boomed, "and that's why we need to get out there as soon as possible—so you and little Aurilla can talk things over while your friends do some fishing." He looked smugly in my direction and winked, and it was the first time I'd ever been proud of my brother-in-law. "We'll pick you up at your place tomorrow morning around six." He pointed at me, catching me in the middle of a gasp. "He'll drive."

"Sounds good," Richard enthused. "Two million bucks, huh?"

"That's a lot of crappie jigs," Thayer said.

"And you'll pick me up at six?"

"On the button," Thayer promised.

"Shoot, guys," Richard said, "I'm too excited to play poker. I think I better go get me a haircut." He grabbed his coat and headed out the door. "See ya in the morning!" The screen slammed behind him.

"Ah-h-h-h, Thayer," I said, rising from the couch. "Didn't you forget something right there at the end? Didn't you forget to tell Richard he was driving tomorrow? Wasn't that what this whole thing was about?"

Thayer rocked back on his heels and grinned cockily. "You don't give me much credit for smarts, do ya, brother-in-law?"

"Well, as a matter of fact . . . ." I tried to collect my thoughts. "That was almost perfect what you did there with Richard," I said. "I mean, you said everything just right until you got to the end and . . . . "

"Brother-in-law," Thayer interrupted, "sometimes I don't think you got so much on the ball, either. Once I discovered Richard was going to inherit Cow Lake, there was no way I was going to let him drive." Thayer shook his head. I thought I heard it rattle. "No, sir. He might of banged up that new vehicle of his and never forgiven us. Why, I had no idea Sutton Grimes had so much land or money, but when Richard let the cat out of the bag, the wheels just started turning, and I says to myself...."

He was still rambling as I slouched out to the garage to break the bad news to the Pinto.

The Primordial Man

When I really want to do nothing, I buy a newspaper, walk over to the Loon Lake Cafe, and sit there drinking coffee and turning pages until I get the caffeine jitters. Occasionally, I'll grunt at the waitress or say "Howdy" to one of the regulars, but mostly I turn pages, keep to myself, and enjoy the relaxing hum of subdued conversations.

Last Saturday, my routine was interrupted. Last Saturday, I glanced up between Ann Landers and the sports page, and I noticed an attractive woman sitting in the booth by the front window whispering to the waitress and pointing in my direction. Well, it has been a fair number of years since an attractive woman, other than my wife, has given me any attention other than to point out the fact my pants were unzipped. I smiled smugly, took up my steaming cup, and holding it carelessly at mouth level in both hands with my elbows resting on the table, attempted to make eye contact. This is a proven method of exuding suave, unless, of course, the steam from the coffee makes your glasses fog up, which is what happened to me. It is extremely difficult to exude suave when your glasses are fogged up.

At the very moment I had decided to abandon my silken image in favor of regaining my sight, the attractive woman pushed back her chair and strode confidently across the room toward me, extending her right hand as she closed the gap.

"I'm married," I croaked, wiping my eyes with a napkin.

"I'm Janene Alonzo," she smiled lustily, still extending her hand. "I write for the *Seattle P.I.* The waitress tells me you're a writer, too."

"Lacey is the only woman for me," I insisted. "Oh, sure, I ran around a bit in my single days, but. . . ."

"The waitress said you did that caribou hunting piece in *Alaska* magazine last year. I remember seeing it on a desk in the news room."

". . .I'm no Casanova, ya know," I continued. "'Course there's some that might tell you different. . . ."

Ms. Janene Alonzo dropped her hand. "Yoo-hoo," she said. "Is anyone home? And did you know you have little water droplets all over your bifocals?" She reached out with both hands, removed the glasses from my head, and began polishing them on the hem of her skirt. "This is a real stroke of luck for me," she said. My *Lifestyles* editor has been wanting a story about modern man's primordial attraction to hunting." Ms. Alonzo sat down across from me, replaced my glasses, pulled a cigarette from a gold case, tapped it several times on the table and put it, unlit, in the corner of her mouth. Then, she produced a note pad. "I suppose it has to do with testosterone and all that."

"I suppose it could," I said. "In my case, however, it has more to do with the trombone."

"Huh?" Ms. Alonzo quit scribbling.

"If I go hunting, I don't have to listen to Herb's kid practice. He lives clean on the other side of the road, but I can hear him plain as day. He's last-chair trombone in the grade school band. Might be better than that someday, but he's still recovering from the incident last winter when he stuck his lips to the fire hydrant by Mike's Tavern."

"Brutal, I imagine," sighed Ms. Alonzo. She cocked her head and looked at me thoughtfully. "Tell me about the pursuit," she said at last. "The chase. Does it stir your soul? Can you feel your roots?"

"Mostly, I feel my ankles and my big toes," I said. "And

my lungs. My lungs burn something fierce when I chase a pheasant through Mrs. Cerenzia's soil bank."

"Well, tell me about that," she said, wiggling toward the edge of her chair. "Two creatures matched in a grim struggle—the hunter and the hunted. A deadly game of wits. What are your thoughts?"

"Actually," I said, "I think a lot about why I miss so much. I wonder why I try so hard to shoot something I have so much respect for, and sometimes I wonder why I don't just go to a nice, quiet bar and watch football."

"And the answer?" Ms. Alonzo asked excitedly. "Is it the blood?"

"If I wanted blood, I'd go to a hockey game at The Arena," I replied. "Or a town council meeting. There are actually two answers, ma'am. One is that I'd rather spend my life in the fields and forests where things still make sense. You and your *Lifestyle's* editor can call it what you want. Two is that there's no such thing as a nice, quiet bar." I gathered up my newspaper and stood up. "Just like today there doesn't seem to be such a thing as a nice, quiet cafe. It's been real special talking to you, ma'am. If that editor of yours is really interested in primordial man, though, have her check out Shagnasty's bar in Deer Park around closing time on a Friday night."

Sneak 707

By age ten, I had already gained considerable notoriety for my outstanding sneaks. I was the only boy in Madison Elementary to ever leave the classroom during Hemo the Magnificent, run to the neighborhood grocery, return unnoticed with corn nuts, and consume the entire package without detection by the teacher. Until Sneak 707, in fact, that single escapade stood in my mind as the epitome of surreptitiousness.

Sneaks were important back then. Sneaking into Mrs. Collett's yard for a capful of raspberries, or Mr. Zimmerman's garage for a look at his waterdogs, was a method of gaining prestige among one's peers. While engaged in these furtive games, one was "sneaking" or "on a sneak," and when bragging about it later, would say he had "snuck" the raspberry patch or the waterdogs. While it is possible neither Mr. Zimmerman nor Mrs. Collett would have been particularly delighted to find us on their property, a sneak was something we did, not something we were.

As I approached junior high age, carrying with me a consuming need to fish, my sneaking became more sophisticated. The nearest fishable water was the creek winding through the municipal golf course nearly five miles from home, and just getting there involved multiple covert techniques. First, I had to sneak my sister's bike from the garage. My sister's bike was always better than my own for long distance trips because mine had been ridden to near-termination playing "polo" in the alley with a cracked croquet mallet and a partially-deflated basketball. Then, I was obliged to sneak past her girl friend's house—

the one who spent hours just staring out the kitchen window so she could rat on me. Next, it was necessary to peddle furiously through several residential areas, trying to avoid the homes of classmates who would never let me hear the end of it if I was seen riding a girl's bike.

Once on the highway out of town, it was easy going until I reached the edge of the golf course where I would hide the bike and slink across the eighth fairway to the creek. From a liability standpoint, of course, the managers of the course could not allow fishing there, but I'm sure the fact I almost always found at least a dozen golf balls—some of them still rolling—had something to do with their inhospitable demeanors. Crouching low, I would duck-walk from pool to pool, drifting my worm beneath the undercut banks and into the mouths of ravenous seven and eight-inch trout. Although I learned later in life that keeping a low profile was actually necessary to both fishing small, clear creeks and surviving P.T.A. meetings, I did it then solely to avoid detection. Nevertheless, a greenskeeper usually spotted me or was informed by patrons of the course of the presence of a large, duck-walking child with a fishing pole, and this always led to a reverse sneak during which I ran like crazy back to my sister's bike.

As I matured, my need to sneak did not diminish. At 16, I had to sneak a new spinning rod into the house because the money for its purchase was supposed to have been spent on school clothes, and a year later, I snuck out of the church at a cousin's wedding, figuring anyone thoughtless enough to get married on opening day of trout fishing did not deserve an audience.

I continued my sneaking ways through college. By then, my tendencies had become too firmly ingrained to discard, and besides, I had certain social obligations and a floor supervisor who didn't allow women in an all-male dorm. Mostly, though, my sneaking involved my appetite for hunting and fishing. In the spring, I would sneak a brown trout, crawling dozens of yards along Crab Creek to drop a fly on his nose. In the autumn, I would sneak anything with fur or feathers that was too far away, too much in the open, or too smart to walk, waddle, swim, or fly my way. During those years, I became friends with Johnny Muskrat and Cynthia.

Johnny was a big, amiable, farm kid from the other side of the state. His real name was Johnny Majeski, and he had earned his nickname trapping a variety of fur-bearing rodents in the sloughs close to campus. Cynthia was a black Labrador retriever, his inseparable companion. Together, the three of us raised sneaking to an art form.

Johnny was just plain fun to be around. He had a theory that people wasted a lot of time arguing and felt if they could eliminate attempts at logic and cut straight to the name-calling, it would save a lot of time. He made up a number code to correspond to his own collection of insults. Thus, once you learned the code, a disagreement would be not only brief, it could be carried on in public places without disturbing anyone. You could, for example, enter the Beehive Cafe, spot an antagonist, and yell across the room, "Hey George—one-fifty-one!" George, in turn, could look up from his coffee and smirk, "Oh yeah? Well, twenty-nine *and* three-oh-three!"

It seemed only logical that Johnny and I would begin numbering our sneaks, also. If we were jumping mallards along the Palouse River and spotted a flock holding against a far bank, one of us could whisper, "Sixty-two," and the other knew exactly what to do. Some time previously, there had been a sixty-two and we remembered. It is possibly worth mentioning here that our numbering system for sneaks was not entirely haphazard. While sixty-two did not necessarily mean there had been a sixty-one or would be a sixty-three, it might have meant there had been six ducks in the original flock and we had dropped two of them.

While juniors, Johnny and I scraped together enough money for tickets to a Safari Club auction and banquet. Though we had no intentions of bidding on anything, we thought it would be fun to rub shoulders, if just for a few hours, with men and women who had snuck African lion, Alaska king salmon, and Montana mule deer.

I have since heard tales of people who have been obligated to pay for an auctioned item after inadvertently scratching their noses during critical moments in bidding. But that's not what happened to Johnny. He tried to justify his purchase of a guided Wyoming sage grouse hunt for two by saying he had blacked out while I was in the restroom and had come to with the receipt in his hand. I, however, knew he had been caught up in the excitement, and what had probably begun as a ten dollar wave "just for kicks" had escalated into a competitive bidding war.

Johnny had always talked about us taking Cynthia to Wyoming some day for sage grouse, and I figured we were fortunate to get off as cheaply as we did. We were even more fortunate Johnny's credit card billing wouldn't come due until we'd had time to hock a few non-essential personal items such as watches, toothbrushes, and most of our school books. Besides paying for our hunt, we needed air fare to Rock Springs, Wyoming.

Considering we had nearly six months to prepare for our Wyoming adventure, Johnny and I should have been pretty much organized by the first week in September, and to tell the truth, we thought we were. Airline tickets had been purchased a month in advance and our guide/host would be waiting at the Rock Springs airport when we arrived on the commuter flight from Salt Lake City. Oddly, I don't remember even discussing just where Cynthia would be kept during the flight. I guess we just assumed she would ride with us.

"You can't have that dog in the terminal, son." The man at the baggage counter was polite as he checked our duffels, but his voice was firm.

"Oh, she's house-broken," Johnny assured him.

"Doesn't matter," the man said. "No dogs except seeing-eye dogs allowed in the terminal."

"Okay," Johnny said, "but what do I do with her until she boards?"

The man looked from Johnny, to me, to Cynthia, and for a moment, I thought he would lose his smile. "Boards?" he said.

"With the exception of seeing-eye dogs, we do not allow canines of any size in the passenger section of our planes. Do you have a certified shipping crate?"

Johnny's jaw dropped in disbelief. He shook his head numbly and backed away from the counter. I looked at the clock. We had 20 minutes until departure. "Can't you call someone to come and get her?" I asked hopefully. "The guy in Rock Springs said we wouldn't really need a dog for sage grouse."

"That's got nothing to do with it," Johnny muttered. "I promised Cynthia we were going to Wyoming. She's been looking forward to this trip as long as we have." He scratched the side of his head thoughtfully. "Take her out front," he said. "I'll meet you there in 15 minutes." With that, he wheeled and strode briskly toward the gift shop.

"Hey," I called after him. "Are we goin' or not?" He didn't act like he heard me, though.

It seemed forever before Johnny returned. "Are we going or not?" I repeated. Inside the terminal, I could hear someone call our flight number.

"Of course we're going," he said. "Sneak seven-oh-seven."

I swished the numbers around briefly in my mind. "We don't have a seven-oh-seven," I said.

Johnny took off his wide, leather belt and secured it around Cynthia's neck. Then he took the sun glasses he had purchased at the gift shop and adjusted them on his face. "We will soon," he grinned, grasping the end of the belt in one hand like a leash. "Sneak seven-oh-seven—you, me, and my guide dog Cynthia on a Boeing 707 to Salt Lake City." He walked slowly, hesitantly, back into the terminal. "Try to get us a seat next to the window, will ya?" he asked. "Cynthia's never been on a plane before."

Gun Walkin'

Until I acquired a brother-in-law, my concept of acceptable adult behavior was rather incapacious. Though possessing a few small flaws of my own, such as a weakness for retrievers and double-barreled shotguns, I had a tendency to judge others according to my own standards of correct and incorrect. Now that Thayer the Abnormal is part of the family, though, I am able to tolerate behavior I would have once called moronic. Thayer, by popular consensus, is at least one slice of bread shy of a sandwich. That's why I didn't say much the other night when I saw him sneaking by the house dragging a shotgun on a length of rope.

"Walking the old automatic, I see," I said casually, as I stepped out of the shadows of the porch. "Good to get them out on a night like this and let them slide around a bit in the gravel."

"Ah, Jeez," said Thayer. "Don't you ever sleep?" He nervously kicked at a steaming pile of lawn clippings by the garbage cans on the road.

"Actually, Thayer, I *don't* sleep much," I said seriously. "I sit by the window all night hoping to see interesting people I can come out and talk to. As none have passed this way tonight, however, I thought I'd talk to you instead."

"Well, I 'preciate that, brother-in-law," Thayer smiled. Then, he looked about guiltily, his eyes fastening on the gun behind him in the gravel. "You probably wonder what I'm doin'," he said.

"It's pretty obvious to me," I quipped, "but some of the neighbors might have a question or two."

Thayer became animated. Shifting his weight, taking a deep breath, and throwing his arms in the air, he began to sputter. "It's a spankin' new shotgun, don'tcha know? I'm tryin' to age it."

"Age it?"

"So's I can get it in the house," he continued.

"Wouldn't it be easier to just carry it through the door?" I asked.

"Ah come on!" Thayer snarled. "You know good 'n well the little woman would hang me by my unmentionables from the porch light if I brought another shotgun home."

"Well, I know *I* wouldn't want to be hung by your underwear from the porch light. And by the way, Thayer, did you ever buy a second pair?"

"We ain't talkin' about my underwear, we're talkin' about shotguns!"

I could tell by his twitching cheek muscles it was time to become a compassionate friend. I had once seen my brother-in-law lift a half-full oil drum into the back of a pickup. What he lacked between the ears, he more than compensated for in brute strength. "I believe I am beginning to understand," I said. "The wife won't let you have a new shotgun, so you're dragging this most recent acquisition in the dirt to make it look old. Then you sneak it into your gun cabinet and nobody will be the wiser. Not bad, Thayer, not bad."

"Thanks," he said. "I thought of it myself."

"It so happens, however," I said, "that I've had a little experience in the matter of gun-aging myself. The object is to rough up the stock a bit, perhaps remove some bluing. What you're doing here could harm the action, knock off the bead, affect the shootability."

"Yeah?" he said. "You got any ideas?"

"Actually, it's quite simple," I admitted. "Leave it with me tonight and tomorrow we'll take it chukar hunting. By the end of the day, you won't even recognize it."

"Chukar hunting?" Thayer's eyes began to roll. "Chukar hunting!" He began to froth. "You mean those little gray buggers with the red beaks? You mean those canyons above the Snake River with all them shale slides and cheat grass and cactus? I said I wanted to age this shotgun, not mutilate it."

"Come on, Thayer," I said. "I go chukar hunting all the time. Do you remember that little 20-gauge of mine?"

"The one with the gouges in the checkering, dents in both barrels, and the missing front bead?"

"Yeah, that's the one. How long do you figure it took me to get it that way?"

"Twenty years?"

"Nope. One season. That's my chukar gun. I bought 'er new last September."

"I ain't going and that's final!" Thayer sputtered. "No way, no how. Don't even ask. Goodnight!"

As I returned to the easy chair beside the front window, Thayer was still on the road, pelting his new gun with handfuls of gravel. Chukar hunting. For a brief instant, I wondered if perhaps it wasn't *I* who was a few pellets shy of a load.

The Christmas Teal

Unlike myself who tried to indefinitely prolong the distressing decision of what to "be" by attending college forever, my son, Matthew, joined the military right after high school graduation. Of course, I viewed this move with no small amount of selfish anxiety; the hunting season was but a few months away, and I liked hanging around duck swamps and pheasant fields with my first born. Additionally, there was the question of who would get stuck with Li'l Dude.

Li'l Dude was a five-month old Labrador retriever, a runt dog purchased with good intentions but minimal forethought when Matt and his girlfriend sloshed into a pet store to get out of a spring cloudburst. He was undersized, clumsy, bullheaded, puppy dumb, and had a penchant for digging and chewing that far exceeded the normal, predictable, puppy penchant. His was an appetite, a fanatical fondness approaching addiction that left the yard of Matt's mother's home looking like a war zone with foxholes, craters, and the mangled remains of flower boxes, plastic garbage cans, bicycle tires, and garden hoses. I already had two hunting dogs, but even if I hadn't, there was no way I wanted Dude.

"Dad," Matt said a week before leaving for boot camp, "Mom thinks Li'l Dude would be happier with you."

I knew what was coming. I had prepared for it, rehearsed my response. Matt's mother and I were no longer married. I suspected *she* really meant she would be happier if Dude was with me, and there was absolutely, positively, not even the remotest possibility I could take care of three dogs. His mother had a country place; at the time, I didn't. Dude belonged with her. "Well," I said, clearing my throat as I arranged my rebuttal, "I've been thinking about that."

"And?" It was not really a question, though—more a plea. Something in it made me recall a ten-year-old boy with an oversized hunting vest, a hand-me-down single shot 20-gauge, and a sidehill covered with pheasants he couldn't hit. It made me remember a freezing December morning and an exemplary stalk through wheat stubble to the Palouse River's edge, and the excitement in his eyes when I indicated with a nod and a grin that the mallards we had seen from the hill were in easy range.

"And I think your mom's right," I said. "Dude belongs with me—with someone who'll take him hunting." And so it was.

During the early grouse season, Dude did nothing to distinguish himself as a bird dog. Mostly, he tagged along with my springers, Sundy and Ami, bowling them over in his awkward exuberance, investigating gopher holes, and contributing his quota of scratches to the pickup door. Well into the waterfowl season, he had still not shown much promise, but in December I decided, nevertheless, to use him alone on future hunts. Sundy and Ami were veterans, and it had been a decent season with numerous flushes and retrieves. Surely they wouldn't suffer too much emotionally if I left them at home and concentrated on the pup. And wouldn't it be wonderful if I could write my son and tell him his dog had retrieved the Christmas goose!

For as long as I could remember, I had never shot more than two geese a year, but always, always, I was blessed with one, which I saved for Christmas dinner. The Christmas goose stood for both the life and the people I loved. Matt wouldn't be home for Christmas, but it would be so fitting if his Li'l Dude could help preserve this special tradition.

The first weekend in December, Dude and I hunted along Dragoon Creek where I had taken four of my last seven geese.

The pup was a little hard mouthed, but made a tolerable retrieve on a mallard drake. There were no honkers resting on the quiet pools, however, a small marsh a few miles away yielded another drake and a satisfactory retrieve.

The next weekend, Dude and I were blanked, and though I wasn't ready to panic, there was some concern. Ice was forming on even some of the larger ponds, and I feared a heavy snowfall would hurry the waterfowl farther south.

By the third Saturday of December—the 17th—my concern was approaching distress. This might be my last chance. On a hunch, I opted for the short drive to a local reservoir.

It was one of those mornings, one of those unexplainable, frozen-digit-but-I-don't-give-a-damn waterfowl mornings when the birds dropped in without circling or even seeming to mind that a clumsy, big-footed, black Lab pup was sitting in plain sight watching them set their wings. On the drive home, with the windshield wipers pushing aside large, fluffy snowflakes, I whistled Christmas songs and planned my holiday menu. Under the canopy of my pickup, Dude lay proudly guarding three mallard drakes, a green-winged teal, and 11 pounds of Canadian honker.

I was in rare spirits as I pulled into the driveway and opened the canopy door, but my *Jingle Bells* died, gasping in mid-pucker when I saw the feathers; Dude had eaten most of the goose.

Red-faced, furious, I seized the mangled carcass by the neck, and wielding it like a wet towel, drove the dog from the truck, chasing him toward the back yard. Dude hadn't even retrieved that goose, swimming instead right by it, becoming entangled in decoy anchor cords, and topping off his slapstick performance by bringing back a chunk of ice! Now he had claimed the bird anyway, and a promise to my son was all that stood between a black dog and a trip to the pound. That evening, I salvaged what I could of the honker, but I didn't feel I could sustain the Christmas tradition with goose chunks. Still, to make the best of a poor situation, I rough-plucked and gutted the ducks and hung them in the shed to age. Four ducks would have to suffice.

On Monday I knew my Christmas dinner was in serious jeopardy when I returned from work and found a pair of mallard wings on the front lawn. The path to the shed was littered with debris—the remains of a Styrofoam cooler, a wool hunting sock, a garden hose with the nozzle chewed off, a scattering of plastic worms from my tackle box, and plenty of feathers. Inside the opened shed, only the teal still hung where I had placed it, and Dude lay lethargically on the back porch, slowly wagging his tail and digesting the Christmas mallards. There was a truck-sized excavation beneath his kennel gate.

One teal. How many Christmas guests could I feed on one teal? I checked the calendar. Christmas was the following Sunday. I would have to squeeze in one more Saturday.

It was 3:30 p.m., December 24, a blustery, no-show day: no ducks, no goose, no Christmas tradition. Sitting on the small, ice-rimmed lake watching me wind decoy cords, Dude perked up his ears when a string of muffled pops in the distance indicated at least someone had gotten some last-hour shooting. I saw him shift slightly and focus his brown eyes skyward, and following his gaze, I spotted a speck in the distance that grew larger and took form as I watched. A goose! A lone honker, a hundred yards up and flying erratically. Undoubtedly hit in the last barrage, he was directly parallel to us above the opposite shoreline when he dropped like a brick from the sky.

Instantly, Dude, that beautiful, lovable, dog-of-my-son's scrambled across shore ice and into the dark chop. With strong, fluid strokes, he paddled toward the other bank, floundering occasionally through free-floating ice, then fighting onward. I watched him at first in open-mouthed amazement, then began to cheer, loudly, rather insanely, throwing endearing words of encouragement across the lake to Matthew's gallant black pup. When his mouth closed firmly upon the Christmas goose, I plopped down, exhausted.

After the feast on Christmas day, friends and family sat lethargically around the warm stove in my front room, sighing contentedly and murmuring softly to whomever was closest.

"Great prime rib, Dad," my daughter, Jennifer, offered as I shoved another log on the fire. "The duck wasn't bad, either. Kinda puny, though," she added. "What was it?"

"Teal."

"What happened to our Christmas goose?" she asked.

I looked at the black pup stretched out by the oven in the kitchen—Matt's dog, Matt's representative at this special celebration. Unlike my springers, he had hardly touched the leftovers, and I smiled despite myself. Twenty-four hours earlier, I had wanted to kill him as he arranged himself comfortably on the far shore of a frozen lake and devoured his second Christmas goose in a week. We had a lot of work to do, that dog and I.

From the Desk of
Alan Liere

Dear Mrs. Scrimshaw:

I am flattered you want me to speak to your Friday evening poetry group, but the truth is, Ma'am, I think you have me mixed up with someone else. No doubt you meant to address Alphonse Learky who, when he's not in detox, lives in an old steam boiler up on Loon Lake Mountain. Alphonse is the one who covers empty wine bottles with free verse written on little squares of toilet paper. Makes a decent flower vase if you're interested. I think the price is $15.95, and part of the money goes to pay for his rehabilitation.

Alphonse and I didn't go to school together or anything like that, but we pass now and then at the post office or mercantile and know one another well enough to say "Howdy." He still says "Peace," though, and smiles at me through the V of two fingers. He remembers 1965 as a great year on Haight-Ashbury, and I remember it as a great year on Seven-Mile Slough. I don't now recall why there was such a mess of ducks moving down the Pacific Flyway that season, but Carlton Hicks and I spent the best part of the winter in hip boots and the worst part anticipating the draft. At the time, Alphonse was tromping around barefoot in bell-bottoms, protesting the government, and picking up Welfare checks. As a matter of fact, that's what he still does. I don't guess you're all that interested in the details, ma'am, but I think Alphonse would be offended if he knew people were getting him mixed up with me.

I must admit I did once aspire to be a poet, Mrs. Scrimshaw, but I guess I wasn't so much interested in a particular cause as in making my friends laugh. My initial attempt was at age eight, but my teacher, Miss Fitz, phoned my Mom and called me some big words. She said if I didn't cease reciting my bawdy "Ode to Miss Fitz" on the playground during recess, she would personally cream me with a medicine ball. She would have done it, too; Miss Fitz once gagged and hog-tied Danny White and made him sit through the entire reading of *Little Women*. It was pretty sad to look over there in the corner and see Danny still trying to be the class clown with only his eyes to work with.

Those were some pretty good years. Miss Fitz had the advantage of being able to verbalize her objections and enforce discipline without worrying about lawsuits, destroying self esteem, or stifling creativity. My Mom, who loved her children more than anything, was extremely supportive—of Miss Fitz. She said if I didn't knock off the playground ballads she'd cut the toes out of my oxfords, paint my toes red, and make me walk to school that way. The threat didn't make much sense, and I suspected it was unenforceable, but it kept me out of the poetry business until I met Davey Crockett.

I may have done a lot better job on that first *Ode* had I waited until the end of my fourth-grade year. Maybe not. By that time, though, I'd discovered books—particularly books about mountain men—and I was able to spice my vocabulary with words like "wagh!, siwash, 'ol hoss," and "booshway." I still don't know what most of those mean, but I sure like the way they sound. Also, "The Ballad of Davey Crockett" became popular that summer, and when school began the following September, I had fanned the creative flicker doused the year before by committing it to memory and adding a few bawdy verses. These, I would sing for my buddies during lavatory breaks. On a dare, I also sang them at the school talent show in December. Let me tell you, Mrs. Scrimshaw, walking to school in the snow with the toes cut out of your oxfords is not that much fun. Red paint provides absolutely zero insulation.

I hope you do not think, Ma'am, that I don't appreciate poets, for I appreciate terribly those few whom I understand. Robert Frost, Robert Service, and Dr. Seuss are my favorites. I think your average poet must be a lot braver than your average dog catcher or even your average meter maid. "Here," he says, "are my feelings. With this poem," he says, "I am putting my butt on the line.". . .Well. . .perhaps that is not exactly the way a poet would say it, but you know what I mean. Robert Frost expressed it eloquently in a letter to a friend: "A poem. . . begins as a lump in the throat, a sense of wrong, a homesickness, a lovesickness. . . . It finds the thought and the thought finds the words." Frost said a lot of other neat things, too, about mending walls and roads not taken and hanging out in a snowy field when you should be home doing the chores. I suspect he was a hunter. That's what I am, too, but I wouldn't mind knowing more about what you are. If you can't get hold of Alphonse, I also wouldn't mind joining your group this Friday. 'Twould add an interesting stir to the soup if nothing else. I'll be the tall guy in camo.

Best Wishes,

Alan Liere

Another Expensive Lesson

Many of my most significant life experiences have been the result of what my father called "getting a hair."

"Getting a hair" is difficult to define, and Dad and I never really discussed its origins. He used the phrase when he was disappointed with me for one reason or another, as in "Every time you get a hair, it ends up costing a bunch of money."

I suspect the definition lies somewhere between profane and esoteric, a transference of body without much conscious input from mind—sort of like the way I did things when I still had pimples. Sort of the way I still do things. "Getting a hair" is to act passionately without forethought on a need you didn't know existed—like digging a trout pond in your yard because suddenly you've decided the epitome of high living would be to catch a trout from the front porch.

"A trout pond, huh?" Lacey grunted. "You want to put a trout pond in the front yard?"

"Yes, dear," I affirmed. "I've been thinking about this a long time." I stood before the living room window studying the slope of the lawn where a couple inches of rain water had collected in a natural gully.

"A long time, as in several years," Lacey asked, "or a long time, as in several weeks?"

"Since breakfast this morning," I admitted, "but I've got a real good feeling about this."

Lacey shook her head slowly and made the soft whimpering noise she always makes when circumstances force her to bemoan the fact there *had been* other men and other proposals of marriage. "You also had a real good feeling about getting that old rototiller fixed," Lacey reminded, "and there it sits with a brand new axle and a brand new transmission. It's the most expensive yard ornament in Loon Lake."

"How was I to know the engine was shot, too?" I whined. "The guy didn't tell me the engine was shot when he was fixing the other stuff."

"He didn't tell you a lot of things," Lacey said. "Like how it would take nine months to get it back or that the bill would be more than the original purchase price."

"Good money after bad," I mumbled. "An expensive lesson."

"*Another* expensive lesson," Lacey said.

"But the pond will be different," I assured her. "It's foolproof. That's solid clay out there. All we have to do is dig a hole. Then, we fill it with the garden hose, put in a pump to circulate the water, and plant fish. What could be easier?"

That same afternoon, I called an excavator, and a week later we had a pond four feet deep, 60 feet long, and 40 feet wide. Three hundred fifty dollars. Then, I read that fish need at least eight feet of water to survive our winters, so I called the excavator back to take out another four feet of soil. Another $350.

Big mistake. At four feet, the pond would hold water. At eight, we had dug past the clay and into sand. "No problem," I told Lacey. "I'll put Bentonite on the bottom and lay heavy black plastic on the sides." That came to $200.

To hold the plastic, Lacey and I hauled in pickup loads of rock—about 80 hours worth, I guess. Then, we shoveled in $160 worth of gravel. My back quit spazzing two weeks later, but I owed the chiropractor for five sessions and was eating Lodine like candy to alleviate the inflammation in my elbows. Medical considerations—about $150.

Next, I bought a small pump for $90, put in an overflow,

and lovingly placed boulders and hollow logs in the pond to provide habitat for the fish.

At last, it was ready to fill, and Lacey and I sat on the front porch the better part of a day watching water from the hose cover the bottom and creep up the sides. This went on for several more days—much longer than I would have thought—but finally our pond was full. I turned on the pump, sat in a lawn chair, and watched the water bubble while I tried to get my check book to balance. It wouldn't, but I was at peace.

In the morning, the pond was only half full. "It will probably take a while to seal," I told Lacey. Still, it disturbed me that the water had drained away faster than it had poured in.

Two weeks later, the pond had been filled five times. Obviously, it wasn't going to seal up on its own. I purchased another $150 worth of Bentonite. No good. I tried laying more black plastic. Still no good.

Three months after beginning the project, I wheeled the old rototiller with the new axle and transmission to the edge of the damp hole in my front yard and pushed it over the side. It tumbled very satisfactorily to the bottom and came to rest in two inches of muddy water. Then, the excavator covered the whole mess with dirt and I planted grass. Another $350. The best money I ever spent.

The Spot

The tree should have never been cut. Most likely, it didn't make the lumber mill in St. Marys. Most likely, it had been reduced to kindling the instant it shot out of that wooden flume and into the big log jam in Hell-Roaring River—another casualty of an inefficient turn-of-the-century log drive. "Will you look at that!" the boss driver probably called. "That big cedar, she don't broom like the white pine; she breaks up. Pity."

"Drop another one," said the foreman. "Maybe the next one'll make it. There's money there if we kin get 'er to town." And they wiped out a 40-acre stand and very little of it made the mill. That was the way of it. There was a lot of kindling in the river that spring, and now, almost a century later, the stump wore its moss coat indifferently.

The old man was sitting there high above the river with his back against that stump. A metal Union fishing rod lay across his lap and he was sucking a cigarette. Home rolled Prince Albert. His features were mostly hidden behind a thick veil of smoke that seemed to have suspended before him.

"Howdy," I offered, trying to conceal my surprise. "Didn't know this spot was taken."

Another cloud of blue-gray smoke rolled slowly upward from his nose, pushing the veil aside. His leathery face was angular and narrow, and only the laugh lines around his eyes kept him from looking pained. "It ain't," he said congenially. He nodded toward another, smaller stump just a few feet away. "Pull up a seat."

Between us, a spring burbled from beneath a granite shelf, filling a pool no larger than a wash tub before overflowing and darting on down the slope. There, it joined another spring with origins higher up the mountain, trebling in volume as it cascaded over a gnarled, mossy root to begin its final descent to the river.

"Kinda surprised to see anyone up here," I said, leaning my fly rod against a blow-down and grunting as I sat. The old man shrugged his thin shoulders but remained silent, so I continued. "There's not many who fish that stretch," I said, nodding down the mountain, "what with the Game Department planting the St. Joe, and all. Too much trouble, and the fish aren't much, either. 'Course what really surprises me is finding someone else in this spot." I swept an arm about to take in the springs and the stumps and all the green goodness about us. "This spot right here."

I was uncomfortable, talking to say nothing, rambling aimlessly. Part of it was jealousy, but there was also anger. This stranger was leaning against my cedar stump. The river below and the mountain above were mine, too. All of it. Ownership by possession. I had paid for the use with sweat. I had paid by giving a damn. Season after season for a quarter century, I had climbed here to eat lunch, tired and hungry after a morning on the big river. Never, never before had I shared it with anyone or even seen signs of use.

The old man studied me through the smoke and smiled. "Ain't been down yet," he said. "Just lookin' for a couple eaters. Those little cutthroat are fine with me." Again, he sucked carefully on the cigarette and I watched him vacantly and thought of another spot I had claimed years before beside the San Poil River in northeastern Washington. There had been a spring there, too, surrounded by fiddlehead ferns, the ground carpeted with knikinik and guarded by towering Douglas fir. After a morning of fishing, I liked to shuck my waders, lie on the cool ground, and be consumed by an unidentifiable euphoria. That spot had been discovered, though, and on my last visit, the red knikinik berries peeked out sorrowfully from beneath cellophane and broken Styrofoam, and the largest tree bore the carved message that Jason loved Michelle.

We sat for some minutes, each absorbed in his own thoughts. The old man seemed nice enough, but damn him! There were thousands of acres. Why did he have to choose mine? I picked up a fir cone and flung it with more obvious anger than intended against a tree. The old man watched the cone ricochet into the cyanothus and the only sound was the trickle of water and a soft exhale like a leaky steam pipe as another cloud of smoke escaped his lungs.

"Somethin' wrong?" he asked at length.

"No. . . I mean. . . Yes," I said. The word surprised me.

"Well?" He wet his thumb and forefinger and crushed the glowing ash of his cigarette. Then, he crumbled it into his shirt pocket and leaned forward, resting his bony forearms on his bony knees.

"It's this spot!" I blurted angrily. "It's mine. This is my spring and that's my stump."

He raised his eyebrows. "Yours, huh?"

"Yes!" I growled, standing. "I've been coming here since I was a young man. Oh, I don't own it or anything, but I wish I did. I feel good up here, mister—alone. Can you understand that?"

Another smile was forming. "I reckon I could if I had to," he said. "You don't reckon it's big enough to share?"

"Hells bells," I said. "Look around. Of course it's big enough. But big enough isn't the problem. I like to see it the way I first remember it—without cigarette butts and candy wrappers and such. I had a place like this once before and. . . . "

". . . some dang fool ruined it," he finished.

"Exactly."

The old man rose slowly, brushing the twigs and moss from his jeans. Stepping over the spring, he extended a hand and I grasped it without thinking why. "The name's Dom," he said. "Dom Vendetti. I own this spot, too." He kept squeezing my hand. "Fact is, I own this whole blessed mountain you're sittin' on and a good piece of everything you can see from here. Got a little place up on top."

He let my hand go and it slapped numbly against my thigh. Then he picked up his fishing rod and turned to leave. "I been comin' to this spot for 50 years," he chuckled, "and I thought *I* was the only one. But you come back any time, son. Any time at all."

Heroes

My father used to say you could tell a man by the heroes he kept. For many years, I judged this a nugget of profound wisdom, the product of deep, philosophical musings, and I let it go at that. A son did not, after all, need to validate what his father had confided. Recently, on a family outing to the beach, I tried, for no particular reason, to share the same intuitive tidbit with my oldest daughter, Jennifer.

"What are you trying to say, Dad?" she asked, flipping up her sun glasses and squinting at me through a copious slathering of baby oil.

"I'm not *trying* to say anything," I grumbled, "I *am* saying it. You can tell a man by the heroes he keeps."

"Tell him what?" Jennifer asked absently, checking her fingernails. "Keeps where?" She pulled a container of bottled water from her beach bag and unscrewed the top.

"Not really *'tell'* him anything," I said, floundering. "More like judge him, I guess. You can judge a man by who his heroes are."

Jennifer studied me sympathetically and nodded. "So who are *your* heroes?" she asked. She took a long draught from the bottle, returned the cap, and put it back in the bag. Then, she rolled over on her beach towel and shut her eyes.

"Hugh Glass," I replied, somewhat surprised at the immediacy of my response. I hadn't really considered the subject for many years—hadn't, in fact, thought of mountain man Hugh Glass since the sixth grade. "He's the only one I can think of right now."

"Cool," Jennifer said, but the way she said it, it didn't *sound* cool.

"Yeah, I guess it would be ol' Hugh Glass, all right," I continued. "Back in the early 1800s, he got chewed up by a sow grizzly somewhere in South Dakota—near the Grand River, I think. He was hurt so bad he couldn't travel and the rest of his party were anxious to get on with their trapping. Eventually, they left him alone to die."

"How rude," Jennifer said. "Did he?"

"Oh, heck no," I replied. "Ol' Hugh finally regains consciousness after about three days. He's not real tickled to find he's been abandoned, but when he discovers his "friends" have also taken his rifle, his knife, and his flint, he's fit to be tied. A lot of men might have given up right there, but Hugh Glass takes off crawling across the prairie, having all sorts of adventures, and eventually he makes his way to Fort Kiowa, two hundred miles away."

"Wow!" Jennifer said. "Look at the size of this mosquito!"

"I knew you'd be impressed," I said, "but what about you, daughter? Do you have heroes?"

Jennifer rolled onto her side and propped her head up with her hand. "Just the usual," she admitted. "Michael Jordan, Brad Pitt, and Hootie."

"Hootie?"

"From Hootie and the Blowfish. He rules."

"But they're all just entertainers!" I protested. "A hero is an individual of distinguished valor admired for noble qualities. Does your Mr. Hootie qualify under those standards?"

"Does anyone?" Jennifer countered. "Does your Mr. Hugh Glass?"

"Most certainly," I said defensively. "You don't think it takes a lot of valor to crawl 200 miles?"

"I think it takes tough knees," Jennifer replied. "After that, I think it takes determination. I do not, however, think you have to be particularly heroic to want to save your skin."

"So where are we now?" I asked, hoping for a compromise. My little girl, I was finding, was a more competent adversary than I had anticipated. For that, I blamed college. "What do *you* think makes a hero?"

"Actually, Dad," she said, "I think a hero is an individual who knowingly risks his life for another individual or a cause. Sort of like you."

"Well, that just goes to show what four years of college. . . . What's that you say? Sort of like me? Are we perhaps onto something here, sweet daughter-of-mine? Are you referring, perchance, to the recent family reunion in Franklin Park during which I drove off the dwarf vagrants attempting to extort money from your Aunt Metabel?"

"Daddy—those were Camp Fire Girls," Jennifer said. "They were only trying to sell a few boxes of mints."

"Well, what then?" I asked. "Certainly not my involvement with your potato salad? I mean, it was out of the cooler for quite awhile, but I don't think it was life-threatening and. . . ."

Jennifer shook her head. "It has nothing to do with the reunion. It has to do with the upcoming Neah Bay salmon opener and the fact I'm graduating in less than a month."

"Yes?"

"They both fall on July 15."

"So?"

"So your friends will think you're a hero if you go salmon fishing instead of to my graduation." She paused for effect. "But Mom and I will kill you."

"Well said," I beamed, "and you know how I detest domestic violence. What, besides bored, will I be if I choose to sit through hot graduation ceremonies?"

Jennifer smiled. "A man of distinguished valor and noble qualities," she said. "Your definition of hero."

"Seems that's the clincher," I said. "Of course I'll be there."

I didn't see any sense in telling her the salmon opener was *August* 15.

Dancin' With Shirley

The pheasant opener would have been better. Had they really known anything at all about hunting and hunters, they would have waited until then to stage their protest. In just two more weeks they might have enlightened mankind and saved all birddom by assembling in the friendly rolling wheat land just south of Spokane. But here? At the bottom of one of the steepest canyons in the Snake River Gorge? They had ventured much to close to the essence of it all.

Like others before them who had joined similar causes, this tiny group of anti-hunters would allow, even encourage, their own exploitation. In the big picture, their protests served only to pad the pockets of the fat cats who headed their organization—the fat cats whose goal was job security rather than victory or even some noble enlightenment. Take on a winless, unpopular cause, gather lonesome, lost, misinformed fanatics as your disciples, fill your coffers with pledges for the "fight," and enjoy the good life. Perpetual employment. Not a bad scheme.

So here they were in Wawawai Canyon with instructions to disrupt the early chukar opener in eastern Washington. Other than that, there were no definitive objectives. Good enough that there was something to stand for. Good enough that they did not have to spend the weekend alone.

Encouraged and directed by a scowling, blustery man in his

mid-60s, a middle-aged fellow wearing a dark beret, a navy-blue tie, and leather street shoes confronted me as I swung from the cab of my pickup. "Do you intend to hunt partridge?" he inquired stiffly.

"Partridge?" I questioned. "You must mean chukars. No one I know calls them 'partridge', though." I pulled my shotgun from behind the seat. "That's what I'm going to do, all right." I glanced critically at his outfit. "How about you?"

The man looked back at the fat cat who was ignoring him and toward others in his group who were approaching a second hunter on the pull-out beside the road. "Sir," he said, "I intend to make sure you have a miserable day."

"Well, that's very thoughtful of you," I said, "but I probably won't need your help. This is chukar country, partner. Look at those hills. In two hours I'll be standing up there on that highest ledge and my tongue will be draggin' the ground right about where you're standing."

"You'll not dissuade me," the man said. "I am sworn to disrupt your hunt. Today, sir, you will not upset the balance of nature. Today, not a feather will fall."

"You must have seen me shoot before," I said. As if to emphasize my deficiency, I stuffed another box of shells in my vest. Then, seeing no need for further conversation, I hefted my 20-gauge and started up the hill. The man scrambled to get ahead of me. "By the way," I called as he stumbled over a field of basalt, "my name is Alan. What's yours?"

"Surely," he said, "you don't expect me to reveal . . . ."

"Then Shirley it is," I said as he huffed and clawed, trying to maintain his balance. "I understand how that goes; had a male cousin once named Karen." I stopped to tighten a boot lace. "But I tell you, Shirley, I wouldn't go scrambling along like that on all fours unless you're immune to snake venom."

The man slammed to a stop, poised like a dog on point. His head jerked around and I could see nothing but white in his eyes. "Snake venom?"

"Western rattlesnakes," I said. "They're pretty pathetic compared to a copperhead or a cottonmouth, but for their size, they pack a real wallop." I picked my way through the talus toward his frozen form. "You might be better off to take it a little slower, Shirley. Maybe you'd be even happier walking along beside me for a spell."

The man pondered my offer briefly. "I know what you're trying to do," he said, "but it won't work. To disrupt your hunt I must stay ahead of you and encourage the partridge to fly. It says so in the manual."

"They don't take much encouraging," I said, "but go ahead if that's what the manual says. Watch out where you put your feet, though, and try to keep your hands off the ground. This is a wonderful dance if the snakes don't get ya. And don't step on your tongue," I added.

Tentatively leaving his frozen crouch, the man made a slow but admirable effort to get above me again, sucking in the sweet morning air and exhaling it noisily as he climbed. When he had gone a hundred yards, I turned to the east and began cutting across the face of the hill to where a patch of wild onions grew. Chukars often went there to feed at first light and I hoped to intercept the first flock before they moved to their rugged loafing areas on the rock faces.

"Hey!" The thin voice echoed down the canyon. "Where. . .are. . .you. . .going?" The words had long pauses between them as if he was having difficulty getting his breath.

"I'm chukar hunting, Shirley," I hollered back. "Remember? I'm out here upsetting the balance of nature!"

"Yeah," he shouted, " but. . .I'm. . .way. . .up. . .here. . .and. . . ."

". . .and I'm not going that way anymore," I finished.

The man didn't say anything for a long time. Then, he got up from where he had sprawled and began slipping across the hillside—on all fours once again. "Wait up," he called hoarsely. It was louder, but the way his words seemed to stick between his lips, I could tell he had cotton mouth.

The sun, which had been only a promise a half hour before, now clawed impatiently at the rim of the canyon. In just a tee-shirt and jeans, I was slightly chilly, but in an hour it would be hot. Broiling hot. And though I hated the extra weight of the two-quart canteen, I would be thankful for every drop before the day was over. I looked down at the speck that had been my truck. I loved seeing where I'd been, smug with the knowledge that the man who can hunt chukars still has some good years ahead.

"Misss-terrr!" A sorrowful call interrupted my reflections. "Could you give me a hand?"

Shirley had taken a shortcut and gotten himself hung up on a rock face. He now hung precariously by his fingertips from a lava outcropping with at least eight feet of air between his soles and the next ledge. Climbing slowly, I edged up beneath him. "Those shoes must be uncomfortable," I said.

"Miss-terrr!" It was pathetic.

"Okay, okay," I said. "I'll have to catch you. Just let go."

"No way!" he whined. "You'll drop me."

"Well, that's a possibility," I said, "but Superman is busy. His sister is getting married this weekend, see, and. . . ."

I caught Shirley around the waist, staggered back a few feet, and recovered without falling. When I put him down, however, he just kept going, melting into an amorphous mass with a silly little beret on top. "So what do you think of chukar hunting so far?" I asked.

The blob moved slightly and a head emerged. It studied my boots several moments, then sat up. He tried to lick his lips, but the tongue was dry and stuck in the corner on the outside of his mouth, and he couldn't speak.

"Sometimes," I continued, "it's even better than this. Sometimes I see huge herds of mule deer. Usually there's a coyote or two, and once I even saw a bobcat."

"Wha 'bout paridge?" Shirley asked, fighting to return his tongue to his mouth. "Dis a paridge hun, iddint it?"

"Chukars," I corrected. "Chukars. I see those, too, but you've got to put in a lot of miles. Shoot, Shirley, we haven't gone more than a few hundred yards." I reached for my canteen and took a sip. Already, the water had lost its icy edge. I offered him a drink which he accepted and which seemed to help him with the tongue problem.

"I think I'll just walk behind you for a time," he said meekly. "I guess I don't need to disrupt your hunt all at once."

"Suits me," I said. "I'll be on my way, then."

Two hours later, I flushed my first birds, and as is my custom, missed badly. A hundred yards behind me, Shirley hollered something quite unintelligible. "What's that?" I hollered back at him. "I couldn't hear you."

Closing the distance between us like a drunk trying to run in a room full of marbles, Shirley threw his arms in the air and shouted incredulously, "You missed?"

"Yes," I affirmed, "I do that quite regularly."

"But I wanted to see a partridge!" he gasped when he finally stopped just a few yards below me.

"Help yourself," I said, pointing down the hill. "They went thataway."

Shaking his head, Shirley plopped down on a flat rock. "Never make it," he panted. "Blisters everywhere."

"That's a shame," I sympathized," 'cause the trip down is worse."

"I was afraid you'd tell me that," he groaned, quietly looking out over the ribbon of water far below. "Kind of like falling down stairs, huh?"

"Not really," I replied. "More like tumbling out of an accelerating truck. How's your forward roll, Shirley? Gymnastic experience is very helpful up here."

Shirley said nothing after that, and we sat silently admiring the view. Several times he shifted uncomfortably and cleared his throat like he was about to start a conversation, but not until I stood to leave did he speak.

"I don't get it," he said. "You climb mountains, you slide, you fall down. Your water gets warm, your lungs begin to burn, and it feels like there's a bonfire in your boots. You walk five miles then miss the only birds you see. How am I supposed to disrupt a hunt like that? It's already disrupted! You don't even care if you shoot a par. . . a. . . a chukar!"

"Oh, I wouldn't go *that* far," I said, "but I've got to admit chukar hunting—any hunting—is a lot like a Thanksgiving turkey; it's the stuff that goes with it that makes it good. I guess you don't really need a gun to chase chukars, but I'd feel awfully silly stumbling around up here without one."

"I know the feeling," Shirley said.

"You might try the want-ads," I suggested. "You could probably get a good used 20-gauge for three-fifty."

"I don't feel *that* silly," Shirley said, gingerly removing a shoe and sock. "This country is magnificent, but I don't think I'll be shooting any chukars." He rubbed his big toe and grinned up at me. "I guess it's not so bad if you do, though."

"That's kind of the way I see it," I said. "You go to your church and I'll go to mine."

Shirley stood up and looked far down the canyon to where an explosion of red-tinted sumac caught the sun. "But maybe we could meet in the middle sometime. Maybe I could follow you around again when my feet are in better shape. Maybe you'd let me shoot your gun once or twice—just to see."

"That's a possibility," I said, smiling. "This is a great dance, Shirley, and anything, don'tcha know, can happen at a dance."

The 'Gar

I quit smoking seven years ago. It was something I'd postponed for three decades, hoping those doctors and scientists and thousands of lung cancer patients would retract the nasty things they were saying about tar and nicotine and other assorted smoky carcinogens. Like Woody Harrelson in the movie, *Kingpin*, I couldn't imagine the American Tobacco Institute standing up for a product that could eventually kill its customers. Just didn't make sense.

The thing is, I really loved smoking. I loved the taste, I loved the smell, I loved the ritual and all the little holes in my shirts and upholstery of my truck. Most of all, though, I loved the intimacy of a smoke-filled room. Nothing could develop camaraderie like sitting around an ashtray with a bunch of confederates who suspected they, too, were slowly killing themselves.

At one time, tobacco—or rather the lack of tobacco—caused me to do some degrading things. In college, I bummed shamelessly. As a young farm hand, I made a corncob pipe, utilizing a rolled up *Reader's Digest* cover wrapped in friction tape for the stem—my first taste of literature. My "tobacco" was either dried corn silk, coffee grounds, or, on a really good day, the crushed, quarter-inch cigarette butts discarded by the itinerant laborers. Even years later, I was not above rummaging through the ashtray for a "keeper" butt and risking lip blisters to smoke it if I ran out of cigarettes at an inopportune time.

I quit because it was something I wanted to do. I quit because my wife thought I couldn't do it. And until I went to

Juneau, Alaska this past summer to fish with friends, I had not been much tempted by the nicotine demon. There had been 2,555 days without a relapse. Tobacco was no longer my master.

The problem began when my friends, Ron Chadwick and John Miller, broke out a package of cigars while trolling for coho salmon just out of Auke Bay, Alaska. "Come on, big guy," they teased. "We're in Alaska, the sun is shining, the salmon are biting, the Mariners are walloping the Yankees on the radio. Only one thing more would make this day complete—a big 'gar."

At first, I resisted. "No way," I told them. "Defective genes. I pick up bad habits too fast." My dad had quit smoking cigarettes for three years and then started again following one after-dinner cigar at a family reunion.

But the pack of cigars was there, and I watched enviously as Ron and John engaged in the elaborate unwrapping, licking, tamping ritual prior to lighting up. The evil seed had been planted. Wasn't everyone smoking cigars these days? Hadn't cigars become the epitome of cosmopolitan recklessness? Couldn't I also prove my strength by smoking just one? Of course I could.

Trembling with anticipation, I placed a cigar lovingly between my lips, anticipating the first acrid bite, the initial "buzz" with which I had been once so familiar. "Light me," I called playfully.

John was fumbling through his many pockets. Ron was searching his tackle box. The contents of a duffel were dumped out and scrutinized thoroughly. No matches! We had no matches! Suddenly, I wanted that cigar more than anything in the world. In 30 seconds I had regressed 30 years—back to the familiar, frantic times I had found myself with cigarette but no match. I was back to the days when I had utilized toasters, ovens, hot plates—anything that would create smoke. At one time or another I had tried rubbing sticks together, striking flint, and during one, most desperate, nicotine withdrawal, had fired off a survival flare. My intent had been to light my cigarette from the flash, but as it turned out, my "rescuers" had a match. As I remember, they also had a nasty word or two.

"Well, I guess that's that," John said, slipping his cigar back into the package. "Can't believe we forgot fire."

"Yeah," Ron grumbled. "Oh well. Let's fish."

"Oh well?" I whined. "Oh well?" Obviously, neither of these men had ever been a smoker. "Oh well" was unfeeling! Draconian! My fingers were trembling. Beads of sweat had formed above my upper lip. How could we fish without a cigar?

"Got any flares?" I asked.

Both Ron and John were eyeing me nervously. Neither had ever seen a smoker suffering from pseudo nicotine deprivation. After conferring quietly as I ransacked the boat for a single match, Ron brought immediate and effective closure: "Al, look," he said, snatching the cigar from my mouth. "All gone!" With that, he tossed both my 'gar and the rest of the pack of five into the sea. The effect was immediate. No matches, no cigar. Once I knew I absolutely couldn't have one, the need disappeared.

Lots of Something

Armed with a homemade spear and fragments of gleaned expertise, motivated more by curiosity than anything, my wife and I recently pulled into the public launch at Eloika Lake. With no visible moon, darkness covered the quiet water like a canvas; we were after bullfrogs.

With Lacey rowing, we swished softly through the rushes, then turned to parallel the shore and a long bed of dollar pads. My flashlight swept to the left and almost immediately picked up a pair of white shining eyes.

"Over there," I hissed, capturing and holding the glint in the beam of light.

"That's a beer can," Lacey hissed back.

"Is not," I said testily. "You think I can't tell a beer can? Row closer!"

Lacey shrugged and maneuvered the boat toward our "prey" until we had narrowed the distance to less than a dozen feet. "You're right," she said in a stage whisper as she peered around me into the water. "It's not a beer can—it's a pop can." Soundlessly then, except for the crinkling of her laugh lines, we slid further into the night.

The next patch of lily pads was at the far north end of the lake, and when we finally arrived, the bullfrog choir was warming up to its performance. Lacey directed the boat toward the enticing assortment of throat-clearing, baritone "ga-lunks."

"There's one!" I said, indicating an unmistakably froggy profile jutting above the lily pads 30 feet off the bow. "Hand me the spear."

There was an unaccountable pause. "Would you settle for a tuna sandwich and some chips?" Lacey asked at last.

"What?"

"Water pack tuna, barbecue chips," she elaborated. "We left the spear back at the launch. Right next to the bucket."

Slowly, I turned to face my wife. Never mind that I'd had nearly 50 years to try frog legs and hadn't, or that the thought of separating them from a frog torso caused an unpleasant quivering in my duodenum. I had the genes of a hunter, and I was, by golly, hunting. "Row closer," I growled, re-focusing both the light and my resolve. "I'll grab him with my hand."

Lacey moved the boat into range. With the flashlight still steady in my left hand, I maneuvered my right above and behind the transfixed amphibian, took a deep breath, held it, and plunged my arm downward. Blindly, then, I retrieved it from the dark water entangled in seaweed and smelling of muck. But the frog was there, too.

"Nice grab," Lacey said. Water ran down my arm and dripped onto my knee and the frog made an uncomfortable "urping" sound. "What now?" she asked. "No bucket, remember?"

"We'll let him hop around in the bottom of the boat," I said. "It's too high and too slippery to escape. Just don't step on him." I released the frog between my feet and smiled triumphantly. "Let's go find another."

By two a.m., the bottom of the boat was covered with a croaking, urping, hopping mass of greenish-yellow amphibians, all of which had received names, and several of which Lacey had at one time or another held at arm's length and communicated with in baby talk.

"Beula likes you," Lacey said playfully.

"Which one is Beula?" I asked.

"The homely one," my wife giggled.

"Very funny. Somehow I never thought of a bullfrog as female."

"Does that bother you?" Lacey asked.

"Not particularly. I just never thought about it. Seems like a contradiction."

Lacey shined the light into the bottom of the boat and smiled whimsically. "Actually," she said, "this whole night has been a contradiction, hasn't it?"

I raised my eyebrows and pretended not to understand, but I did. A portion of my primordial instincts had temporarily abandoned me at mid-lake.

"This was fun," Lacey continued, "but there's no way I can eat frog legs now. I mean, we've practically shared recipes. Geraldine, here, wants you to be a Godfather." She gathered up one particularly large blob of friendly frog flesh from the bottom of the boat and held it tenderly at arm's length. "We have to let them go, you know. Maybe we can do this again another night. I think on another night with the spear and all, it would be better. Don't you?"

"It was fun, dear," I admitted. "Lots of fun. Lots of something, anyway. But I doubt we can do it another night, either."

Lacey nodded, extended her arms over the water, and opened her palms wide. Geraldine urped gratefully and did a belly flop back into Eloika Lake. Not as impelling, perhaps, as the release of a wild steelhead, but satisfying nevertheless.

86   Dancin' With Shirley

From the Desk of
Alan Liere

Dear Steve,

We're home, but I don't know if that's good or bad. It's considerably cooler in these parts than it was in Ft. Lauderdale, and neither Lacey nor I are adjusting very quickly. A sun tan, we're discovering, is not nearly as effective as Thinsulate for holding in body heat.

We ignored your advice and went to DisneyWorld before flying out of Orlando. I think you and those Southern Baptists may be onto something, Steve. Folks we talked to said it would take two days to do the Magic Kingdom and three to do EPCOT. Lacey and I did each of them in 8 hours, and that was too long. I guess we're just not Magic Kingdom types. I hate lines, I hate crowds, and I hate paying three bucks for an ice cream cone. I loved the manatees, but Snow White ignored me.

Other than that, our trip to Florida was perfect and we want to thank you and Sharon again for the southern hospitality and the great fishing! That bonefishing trip out of Bud N' Mary's Marina off Islamorada in the Keys was like a fantasy come true. (I know, I know—you have your fantasies, I have mine). I'll be sure to write Capt. Stanczyk a letter, but should you see him anytime soon, tell him I dreamed about him last night. . . .On the other hand, just tell him thanks. He mentioned he'd like to do some duck hunting up this way next winter. I don't want to scare him away.

Don't forget to give Tom Calandra a copy of the enclosed recipe for pickled fish. That light tackle trip off his *T&M's Dusky* was another vacation highlight. Who would have believed I'd actually hook a tarpon my first time out! And a 65-pound sailfish on 12-pound test line? No way. I'm so glad you took pictures before we released it because everyone I tell that story to says I have the numbers reversed. Tilly Shuck caught a two-pound bluegill on 14-pound test off her dock this spring and they tried to make her mayor of Loon Lake.

Also, Steve, please tell Capt. Mallet that Lacey says she's going to start lifting weights in preparation for our next offshore trip to Florida. We sure would have liked to have seen what it was she hooked aboard his *Just Add Water*, but I guess any fish that can fight that hard and stay down that long deserves to go on swimming. Lacey's been telling everyone it was a marlin, and it may have been, but Capt. Ron's theory about a huge snook or foul-hooked barracuda seems plausible, too. Incidentally, we used your recipe and blackened some of the yellow jack fillets for dinner tonight. Delicious!

Now that you've shown us some real fishing, I think you and Sharon had better make plans to spend a couple weeks here next fall so I can show you what real waterfowl hunting is like. I just can't imagine having to include sun block and mosquito repellant with my duck hunting gear. Waterfowling is a cold weather sport, buddy! Your nose is supposed to turn red and drip. That's half the fun! The other half is the dog work. After what I saw while tooling the back roads of Florida, it's a wonder to me there are any dogs left! I tried to retrieve a downed pheasant from a hog pen once, but there's no way I'd do the same for a duck in an alligator hole.

If you come up, we'll have to spend at least two days on the west side hunting sea ducks. Mike and I tried it last year for the first time, and now he's talking about making it an annual pilgrimage. Last year I developed a crick in my neck trying to keep up with all the birds flying through our decoys. You know, I thought I was fairly adept at waterfowl identification, but there are ducks over there in the Pacific Ocean I've never even seen pictures of. By the end of the first day I was calling them all "brown ducks." By the end of the second day, I had refined my system somewhat, identifying more specific varieties such as brown-and-white ducks, black-and-brown ducks, big-brown-ducks-with-a-touch-of-orange, and little-brown-and-white-ducks-you-can't-hit-no-matter-how-far-you-lead-them. On day three, for the sake of brevity, I went back to "brown ducks." It didn't help the crick, though. Or my shooting.

We had a storm here the day we got home, and it was a doozie. It paled in comparison to the ones we experienced daily in Florida, however. Florida thunderstorms are like a healthy marital spat—the kind that erupts with electricity, clears the air, and leaves the relationship clean, refreshed, and drenched with sun. When nasty weather comes to these parts, it likes to hang around, kick the dog, and feel sorry for itself. This was a particularly wet year in eastern Washington—great for ducks and raspberries. Incidentally, Lacey wants to send you some raspberry jelly, but I told her you probably had your heart set on choke cherries. In any event, feel free not to reciprocate; Florida mangoes are highly over-rated.

My best to Sharon,

Alan

I'll Just Sit Here and Read

There is an unwritten law which says the greater the need for anything, the less your likelihood of obtaining it. Love and clean underwear come immediately to mind, but sleep is even more elusive.

It is unnatural that *Homo sapien* has assumed an upright stance, and walking, in itself, is an absolutely ridiculous and stressful mode of conveyance. To do so over hill and dale and through briar patch and swamp is insane. Without a good night's sleep, it is impossible. One *needs* a full eight hours the night before he goes hunting.

Ordinarily, I have no difficulty getting to sleep. Most nights, I begin dreaming at approximately the time my right leg is withdrawn from my trousers, and until the alarm clock or my wife beseeches me to get up and do something with my life, I remain oblivious to all nocturnal happenings. On weekends from September through mid-January, however, I can't buy a night's sleep, and it has been this way since I shot my first pheasant in 1962. If my calculations are accurate (based on an average of 17 hunting weekends per season), that is 9,792 hours of lost sleep since I first picked up a shotgun.

Being of an analytical nature and, as my wife maintains, "a few tomatoes shy of a box," I have devoted some study to the phenomenon of sleepless Fridays and Saturdays during the hunting season. The accumulated data is much more complicated than I would have imagined. Isolated elements work singularly or in combinations, but it is now obvious that **NORA** is the culprit.

NORA is *not* my great aunt—that's Cora. Although Cora *did* once insist on showing the slides she'd hired a fellow to take while the dentist cleaned her teeth, thereby keeping me up well past midnight on the eve of a mule deer expedition, she isn't normally around that much. **NORA** stands for **N**eed, **O**rganization, **R**itual, and **A**nticipation, a combination of emotions and procedures that keeps my sandman at bay during the hunting months.

The first of these, **N**eed, has already been mentioned. The more one needs something, the less accessible it is. I can crawl into the house on a Friday evening, exhausted after a 14-hour workday, knowing that in the morning I will drive 120 miles to hunt sidehills from dawn 'til dusk. "I need to get some sleep," I'll tell my wife. Big Mistake! The mere thought that I *must* rest will keep me awake all night worrying about it, trying to force it, willing it to come.

Organization is the bane of many. For me, it has never happened. "Is the 20-gauge in the gun rack with the 12, or is it still in the basement with the canteen and fanny pack? Where did I put the turkey call? How many sandwiches should I make? What?...We're out of bread!... How long is the store open?... I could have sworn the wool socks were in the same drawer as the long underwear... Whaddaya mean they're still in the wash?" By the time I have gathered my gear and stacked it neatly by the door, the night is shot and I'm too wound up to sleep anyway... Three a.m.?... "Might just as well sit here and read."

Ritual is also a thief of sleep on the eve before the big day. I always clean my gun and grease my boots the night before, and it doesn't matter that it was already done immediately after the last outing. I must also remove every shell from my vest loops and reinsert them just so. That done, the dogs will need a pep talk. Then, there is the ritual of breakfast which, incidentally, becomes more important (and longer) as the years go by.

Meeting friends for breakfast means getting up an hour earlier. If I haven't seen them for a few weeks, I'd better figure on *two* hours. It takes a long time to drink 12 cups of coffee and tell all my accumulated lies. Heck, I'll have to get up pretty soon anyway. "Might just as well sit here and read."

Anticipation is like the late bird in a covey of chukars; it's always there to jump up if other emotions and procedures have somehow avoided me and a good night's sleep seems imminent. Replays of frost-tipped stubble and long-spurred roosters, the smell of corn silage, and the comforting recoil of a smooth-swinging double, dance on the popcorn ceiling. "How can you even think of sleeping?" they say. "That little eyebrow of wheat grass above O'Donley's barn will be crawling with quail at first light, and it's certain the Huns are back in Mrs. Moberley's cottonwoods." At 2:30 a.m., having rolled over 237 times, I get up and dress. Breakfast is at four. It's too early to warm up the truck. "Might just as well sit here and read."

The Dog, Walter!

One day in the spring of my third year at college, while sitting in a campus laundromat watching my socks go around and reflecting on why I was failing both English *and* Badminton, I noticed an ad on the bulletin board for Brittany spaniels.

The asking price was $50, but I offered $25—a figure I arrived at by carefully calculating the animal's lineage, conformation, and the amount of money in my savings account. He for sure wasn't a field champion, but he *was* a hunting breed, and though he would complicate my life and was probably still over-priced, I snuck him into my dorm and named him Britt. A week later, he had pretty much destroyed the 11th floor of Pierce Hall, and I took him home.

My father, as was his custom when he heard my car in the driveway, was hiding behind the couch. He had somehow gotten the notion that college was an institution of learning and was so disappointed his only son viewed the time away from home as an extended holiday, he avoided me whenever possible.

"I have some really great news, Dad," I said, pulling my laundry bag to its customary spot in the middle of the living room floor. "I bought a hunting dog."

I heard a soft whimper from behind the couch. "A dog?" Dad finally moaned. "My son the scholar bought a dog to help him pass English?"

"It's a Brittany spaniel, Dad," I said cheerfully. "He can help next semester when I take that European Poetry course." My father said nothing. "They won't let me keep him in the dorm any longer," I continued, "so I've decided to move back home and commute."

My mother, of course, was delighted her baby would forsake the temptations of dormitory life and return to the nest. "Walter," she said emphatically, "you stop moaning like that back there. We'll build a nice pen in the backyard and you'll never know he's around."

"We can keep him in a pen?" my father questioned, rising to one knee.

"Of course," Mom comforted. "You don't think I'm going to have him running all over the neighborhood, do you? The Van Dykes would have a fit if he ruined their roses."

Her words seemed to make Dad feel a little better, and he hauled himself upright. "Wel-l-l," he said slowly, "I don't think he'd do that. I mean, he isn't the most perfect son in the world, but we *did* teach him to respect the property of others and. . . . "

"The **dog**, Walter!" Mom shrieked. "I'm talking about the dog! You two get over to Bob's Hardware and buy what you need for a pen."

Actually, my father didn't dislike me. Before high school and college, we had spent many pleasant years together. Eventually, my resistance to higher education became a source of irritation to him, but on a scale of one to ten, I was a solid six. Though he had happily lengthened the apron strings when I went off to make my mark as a professional college student, I think he would have tolerated my presence home again had I not brought Britt. Dad took tremendous pride in his city lot, had developed an iris bed that was the envy of the neighborhood, and maintained a lawn with nary a blade out of place. He'd never had a dog, and Britt certainly didn't fit into Dad's landscaping needs.

By late spring, the iris were gone—chewed off just above the roots. Though I kept Britt in his kennel when I was in school, I couldn't bear to see him locked up when I was home. The lawn, once such a perfect, uniform color, was splotched with browns, yellows, and tall fringes of green. Then, as he matured, Britt began marking his territory from three legs rather than a squat, and it wasn't long before the shrubs, also, began to look sickly. This, and the foxholes he created burying bones and searching out enticing smells, gave Dad's *Better Homes and Gardens* yard the appearance of a war zone.

In early September, Mom suggested Dad had reached the end of his rope. "Son," she said, "I know how much you love that dog, but I've developed an affection for your father over the years, and I'd like to keep him around."

"You want us to leave?" I asked, lower lip trembling. "You want Britt and me to find a house on campus?"

Mom shoved a chocolate chip cookie into my mouth. "Quit your blubbering!" she said kindly. "I do **not** want you to leave. I want you to take your father bird hunting. Show him that dog's got some worth."

At first, Dad complained a lot and said he didn't want to know about shotguns, but I talked him into some trap shooting, and he was pretty good. In the weeks just before opening day, I thought I could detect a degree of anticipation, and in the evenings, he would sometimes lay aside his *Sunset* and pick up my Cabela's catalog. He still cringed, though, when he went near his iris bed, and Britt was still viewed with contempt.

On opening day, Dad got all trembly and weak-kneed and babbled like a little kid when he missed his first pheasant, but toward the end of the afternoon, he dumped a rooster on the fringes of a corn patch—a bird Britt had pointed. We searched 20 minutes for it, the dog coursing madly back and forth and finally taking off down a row, stretched out like a greyhound. Dad was sitting dejectedly on the lip of an earthen irrigation canal chunking dirt clods at a tumbleweed when Britt trotted proudly from the corn forest carrying that bird.

"Well bless your heart," was all Dad said as he accepted the gift, but I knew he was hooked. The following Monday, he moved his iris to the front of the house, tore down the kennel, and fenced in the entire back yard. It had taken both of us too long to get our first dog. We certainly wanted him to feel welcome.

Eatin' Dust

An outdoor writers' organization I belong to holds its annual meeting each year in the Press Room at Seattle's Kingdome. For those of you who only suspect you know outdoor writers, this must seem to be just too much fun, and I assure you we are a bunch of wild and crazy guys.

For two riotous days, we drink coffee (black), eat donuts (brown), and watch videos in which salmon spawn, turkeys strut, and slow-motion bullets are shot into huge blocks of wiggling gelatin. We also hear speakers discuss methods of composing query letters to outdoor editors, organizing files, and overcoming the twin debilities, "writer's block" and "writer's butt."

At the end of this wanton weekend, those of us still awake assemble around a garbage can full of tickets where 5,000 hand warmers and a million spools of coffee-colored monofilament will be raffled off one at a time. This, as you might imagine, causes a great deal of excitement and anxiety among the 52 attendees, and the competition is keen.

This year, we have a new president, and in an attempt to inject additional substance into our meetings, she introduced the concept of craft improvement seminars. Now, I have a fishing boat, a fold-up boat, a duck boat, and a canoe. All of these crafts are in pretty good shape, none are in need of improvement, and you can imagine that I did not take kindly to a seminar that was going to interfere with the salmon spawning video.

When our president explained the seminars were not about

boats and would indeed help me earn more money in my chosen *craft* as an outdoor writer, I was still skeptical. The word "more" indicated she thought I was already making money. The truth is, the life-long ambition of every outdoor writer out there is to win a twenty-million dollar lottery and then write like crazy about fishing and hunting until the money's all gone.

Eventually, I agreed to try staying awake through the craft improvement seminar on digital cameras. God knows my pictures need help. For as long as I can remember I've been told the camera is an outdoor writer's best friend. For as long as I can remember, I have been told that excellent photography will sell the outdoor story much quicker than excellent writing. That is why I usually try to write humorous stories which require *no* photography; I am not even adequate with a camera, and there is zero market for humorous photos.

The seminar I attended was presented by a young man from Seattle named Jim Miotke. He seemed like a nice-enough fellow, but I'm pretty sure he had a brain disorder, because he didn't say one complete sentence I understood. Sometimes, I could make out a word or two, but the thoughts just weren't coming through. He'd start out and I'd be doing just fine, and then he would lapse into gobbley-gook and say something like "Anytime you save in J-Peg, the resolution will munch down." After that, he'd say a bunch of numbers. Three, ten, 500, and 120 were some he used a lot, but he seemed partial to 72.

At one time, Mr. Miotke suggested I could output an 8x10 at 300 dots per inch but I might run into pixtelation problems. A short time later, he said something about "digitizing yourself," and that's when I stopped listening altogether. If Mr. Miotke wants to digitize himself, that's his business, but I still have a lot of faith in Dr. Corbett.

Some of my colleagues, I noticed, were asking questions, and I must admit this bothered me some. My colleagues' apparent ability to comprehend gobbley-gook and changing technology has always bothered me some. WHAT HAPPENED TO ME? In high school I used to pretend I knew what was going on in class by asking questions. Sometimes, I'd come out of a pheasant hunting dream, wipe the drool from my desk, raise my hand, and say, "Do you think Caesar suspected the conspiracy?" Mrs. Greymouth would shake her head and cluck sympathetically, "This is Geometry, you bird-brain."

The nasty thing about today's ever-changing technology is you can't even *try* to fake it. If you raise your hand and start asking questions about megabytes, gigabytes, and snakebytes, you better have a clue. Having Jenny Smart in homeroom laughing at your dumb questions was one thing. When the editor of some outdoor magazine is laughing, you've lost a market.

My brother-in-law, Thayer the Abnormal, suggests I am being left in the dust of technological expansion because I refuse to abandon my childhood. A digital camera, he explains, requires no film and the pictures it takes are instantly accessible by plugging the camera into a computer terminal. Oh sure, your burst rate is slower with a digital and the low price range is still four figures, but just imagine gaining the capacity to convert your pixtel to DCI!

Just imagine, I tell him back. Just imagine an old box camera, your first roll of Kodak, and a long summer day to do nothing with but waste. Ain't no digital could be better than that. And that's why I'll always be eatin' dust.

This Kid

Fighting both incline and October wind, my camper chugs to the summit of Lookout Pass. Montana is on the other side. A faded, green tuna boat zips by with a friendly honk, and a girl of about 14 waves at us through the back window. "Geez, Alan," my stepson says, ducking his head from her view. "You gonna let everyone pass ya?"

I try to smile, but don't quite bring it off, then try again to remember what it was like to be 15. With Evan, it seems I'm always trying to remember what it was like to be younger, but I never quite bring that off, either. "She's not hauling a camper with two dogs and provisions for a five-day bird hunt," I finally say, and Evan sits up and peers into the rear-view mirror. "Here comes another one," he moans. "A '79 Pinto." He rolls his eyes. "We're gonna be passed by a friggin' Pinto."

"Watch your tongue!" I tell him sharply.

Evan looks at me in disbelief. "For 'Pinto?'" he says sourly.

"For 'friggin'."

"'Friggin' isn't a cuss word."

"It's close enough," I say angrily. "Keep it to yourself."

On the down side of the mountain and into western Montana, Evan keeps it to himself. Highway 90 pulls us along in uncomfortable silence, the landscape dominated by pine and fir and a few fields of yellowing alfalfa that appear to be losing their struggles with the native vegetation. We stop for gas in Missoula, and while I clean windows and check the oil, Evan dashes inside to begin flicking through a rack of hot rod magazines. I glance at him and shake my head. Hot rod magazines!

At his age I could think of nothing but hunting and fishing—and maybe a girl now and then. But I wouldn't have looked at a hot rod magazine in a million years, and if my father had offered to take me along on a trip like this, I would have been polishing the hubcaps when we stopped for gas. And that's the way *my* son, Matt, had been, too. But this one, I thought. . .this kid. . . this kid's no damn fun.

I slam down the hood and go inside to pay. Evan looks up and I motion it's time to go. Carelessly, he tosses the magazine back onto the rack and heads for the lavatory.

"Shouldn't you have done that when we got here?" I growl. He frowns and jerks his head around but says nothing, and disappears down a hall.

Butte, Bozeman, Billings. Two hundred miles of Big Sky and cold sunshine. Then we are under heavy clouds and it begins to snow. Evan cracks his window and pushes his fingers through the opening. "Is this what we're going to hunt in?" he wants to know. "It's cold out there." Not exactly a whine, but a complaint to be sure. It's the first time in four hours he's had his headphones off.

"I guess we'll take what we get," I tell him, "but I wouldn't think this could last. It's only...what?... the seventh of October?"

"The eighth," he tells me. "When we gonna eat?"

The Cattleman Cafe in Billings has the best beef in the state. It was a tradition with Matt and me to blow the budget the first night out in Billings, then do our own cooking the rest of the trip. Evan and I slide into a booth near a window where we can keep an eye on the camper. The waitress comes and I order prime rib and coffee. "Matt always had the T-bone," I tell Evan.

"I'll have a chicken sandwich and fries," he says. "And a hot chocolate." He peers out into the swirling snow and drums his spoon absently on the edge of the table. "We gonna keep drivin' in this stuff?"

"Let's get some sleep and get after it early in the morning," I say.

"A motel?" Evan asks hopefully. "With a TV?"

I shake my head but forget again to smile. "This is a camping trip, kid. Remember? I'll pull onto a side road after we eat. Make sure you use the bathroom before we leave." No instinct whatsoever, I am thinking.

Evan had been 13 when his mother and I married—the same age as my son, Matthew, when *his* mother and I divorced. As I had done with Matt, I introduced Evan to spinning rods and BB guns immediately. I've always thought a boy needs stuff like that to grow up right. I hadn't, however, bought him a shotgun until just recently. This would be his first real hunt, and I was anxious to see how he would respond. Perhaps in hunting we could make the connection. Evan seemed to have a genuine interest in the outdoors, though he lacked much of the intensity I had passed on to my son, and he frequently said and did things that got on my nerves. For me, our excursions afield were oft-times undertaken more out of a sense of obligation than anything. I would have rather been by myself. Or with Matt. Perhaps especially with Matt. And now, on our first hunting trip, I am also disappointed that Evan doesn't seem particularly excited. It just isn't the same with this kid with the different last name.

We awake to a promise of sunshine. Outside, only a trace of the early snow still lingers. We eat cold cereal and donuts in the camper and are on the road by 7:30, still pointed eastward—past Pompey's Pillar and Custer, past Forsyth and Hathaway. Just beyond Miles City we leave the four-lane and get on Highway 12 to Baker. Evan has stashed his headphones and his nose is pressed tightly against the window. We begin to see small herds of antelope. At Baker, we turn onto Highway 7 and take a two-lane roller coaster ride over red caliche, south toward our destination in Ekalaka, Montana. Evan comments on the friendly two-finger waves from the driver of every approaching pickup. It reminds me of a story, and I tell him a joke about a man called "Three-finger Willie." He misses the punch line, though, and doesn't laugh. Matt had laughed.

The landscape is dry, dominated now by sage brush and

CRP, though there is a fair amount of wheat stubble. We roll by a half-acre stock pond surrounded by antelope and then the honeycombed, sandstone Medicine Rocks where Chief Sitting Bull came to consult with his spirit. A state policeman pulling a horse trailer passes us and Evan giggles. "Only in Montana," I tell him.

We pull into Ekalaka, Montana, after lunch. It seems most of the 1,119 residents are on their way to the high school gymnasium to watch the Ekalaka Lady Bulldogs play the Broadus High Lady Hawks. We join the migration, looking for friends, Jerry and Betty Cline, whose oldest daughter, Mikal, is a starting point guard for the Lady Bulldogs. Evan and I sit with them and watch the home team nurse a small lead through four quarters. I am excited, but Evan is more animated than I have ever seen him. "I didn't know you liked basketball so much," I say, nudging him with an elbow.

My stepson grins. "I didn't know you liked it at all," he said.

"I guess I never mentioned it."

After the game, Jerry spreads a section map out on the fender of his pickup and shows us where to find sharptails. He has access to several thousand acres near Ekalaka, and though he doesn't have the numbers of sharptails I have seen in Alberta and other parts of Montana, we have a great place to camp and there are always enough birds to make things interesting. We choose a spot, say good-bye to the Clines, and return to the truck. It won't start.

"Pop the hood," Evan says, getting out.

"Yeah, right," I say sarcastically, but I do it anyway. There are no mechanic's genes in my ancestry. What goes on under a hood is magic.

"Try it now," Evan says after only a minute. The engine roars to life.

"Don't even tell me," I grin when he slams the door and settles back into the seat. "I wouldn't understand." We drive to our spot, an abandoned homestead, let the dogs out of their kennels for a romp, and set up camp. We will hunt in the morning.

At dusk, we are drawn from our dinner by a strange, eerie chirring noise, and we watch as four distinct waves of large birds pass high overhead. I'd never heard anything like it.

"Some kind of geese?" I wonder out loud.

"Sandhill Cranes," Evan says. His mouth is open slightly and his head is tilted back, as if he is drinking in the sound.

"You sure?" I have never seen a sandhill crane.

"I've seen them on TV," he responds almost dreamily.

"I thought you just watched those goofy sit-coms," I say.

Evan smiles and shrugs his shoulders, and we stand silently together to marvel at the rest of the show.

At daybreak, we are enduring the thorns and wind as we fight through a grove of Russian olive. Then, eighty yards to our right, Evan spots a dozen birds feeding in the open in a dry pasture. Sharptails.

I heel the dogs and we crouch down to watch. "We're not likely to get much closer," I tell him finally. "Right now they don't know we're here, but as soon as they see us they'll be gone."

"What if I can crawl to that post?" Evan is shaking with excitement as he nods toward a sagging hog wire fence 20 yards into the pasture.

"You'd never make it without being seen," I tell him, "and that's not really the way we hunt birds, anyway. Let's let the dogs go and see what happens." I watch his eyes darken as the disappointment seeps in. "The fence is still too far," I say at last. "You'd have to crawl through it and then another 30 yards besides. There's not much cover out there."

"Can I try?" he asks. He has flattened out on the ground with his shotgun cradled in his arms before him. His whole face is pleading "Just let me try."

I shake my head no, but wave him on. Even for a futile cause, I appreciate enthusiasm. "Good luck," I say with a hint of sarcasm.

With his face in the dirt, Evan begins to crawl. He slides out of the row of trees and into tall bunch grass. I can follow his progress by an almost imperceptible movement of the stalks. Before I know it, he has spanned the distance between me and the hog wire—but still 30 yards from a good shot. He'll have to go over the fence, and that will be the end of it. I see his head come up slowly, then back down, then reappear 20 feet away. Again, he disappears, and the next time I see him, he *is on the other side of the fence!*

"Well I'll be damned," I whisper.

Then, Evan is up and charging, and I am up too, and the dogs are on their way. I see the first bird break and Evan stops and raises his shotgun. Then the entire flock has caught the wind and is peeling away. Still, I flinch at the shot, which seems to come too soon.

"Did you get one?" I yell. Evan is running across the pasture, and before I have cleared the hog wire fence, his whoops tell me he has.

He protests mildly as I smear his forehead with the blood of his first kill. "It's a tradition," I tell him. "It's to honor both the animal and the hunter." I start to shake his hand, but it doesn't seem appropriate, and I put my arm around his shoulder instead and squeeze. Again, I am wondering what it is like to be 15, but this time I remember just a little. I am thinking, too, that part of what has been wrong with Evan is really wrong with me.

The Curse

My immediate family and all living relatives are respectable folks of adequate intelligence and phenomenal longevity, still in possession of at least half the mental faculties with which they were born. I have cousins that teach, nephews that preach, and a niece who knits sweaters from dog hair. There must, however, have been some peculiar characters in the woodpile of my ancestry, for how else can I account for the way I am?

I've heard that my great, great, Uncle Beamer was involved in a land dispute with the first state governor, and my grandmother still whispers at family reunions about an unnamed female cousin from territorial days with an occupation in the "late-night, adult-entertainment field." Another cousin twice removed and once hanged was a "livestock broker" in the 1890s, specializing in longhorns that didn't wear his brand, and yet another cousin made and lost a couple fortunes, and then a liver, during Prohibition. But I'm not talking about those kinds of characters.

There is an undeniable presence in my genealogy of subsistence gatherers—men or women who lived from hand to mouth—individuals who never let pass an opportunity to take game or fish or berry or nut because they didn't know how long it would be between meals. And out of the myriads of aunts and uncles, cousins and great cousins who *could have* been passed the gene, only one was cursed.

Why I, conceived after the Depression, schooled during the space race, and dumped into a modern technological society should retain primitive gathering and hoarding instincts, is a source of both puzzlement and concern. Why do I, a city kid raised on TV dinners and Spaghetti O's by good American consumers, now look at those who eat such fare not so much with distaste as with sympathy? While my friends and colleagues are booting up, going on-line, exchanging e-mail, and trying hard to become good cybercitizens, I'm outside scrounging the woodlots for mushrooms or collecting rose hips for jelly. While they make "civilized," semi-weekly pilgrimages to the supermarket and call it a "good day" if they find a parking place right out front, I'm gathering pine nuts on Pease Mountain and experimenting with methods of cooking freshwater mussels so they do not have the texture of pencil erasers.

I'm out of place in this century because I derive immense satisfaction in putting food on the table that is not boxed, canned, fortified, frozen, or sold by the pound. And it's not the money—it's something much more compelling—something I *have* to do. One can buy lobster for 16 dollars a pound and get something good every time. A pound of crawdads requires an hour of driving, two hours of catching, and three hours of cleaning. Then, maybe—just maybe—they'll be worth eating.

I am not a weekend sportsman. This is not to suggest I cannot enjoy catch-and-release fishing, or hunting for the pleasures kindled by being physically active in field and forest. This is not to suggest I need a full stringer and a heavy game vest to have a good day afield. Indeed, I probably eat no more *ordinary* fish and game than the next sportsman. My problem lies in an obsession for culinary experimentation, a proclivity for setting my table with the unusual.

It goes something like this: I'm grouse hunting along Chimmikain Creek and I happen upon a small patch of wild currants—a very small patch of wild currants. Still, I'm thrilled because it's late in the year and the season is long past. I had not expected to find currants again until the next July.

I lay my shotgun aside and half-fill a sandwich bag I find in my game vest. Then, I look around. A cup of currants is hardly enough for a sauce, but there has got to be more somewhere close. Two hours of intense searching, during which I erase all thoughts of baked grouse, proves me incorrect. There are no more currants—but no matter. I have discovered shaggy mane mushrooms growing near a rotting cottonwood stump and I've soon gathered enough to suffocate my next wild turkey roast and provide some additional, nutty texture to a future batch of venison stew. The next day is Monday, but the boss is out of town and things are usually slow at the office on Monday. I take the day off and return to Chimmikain Creek to lay in a supply of mushrooms for winter. Alas, that single cottonwood stump was the only one in the area. There are no more edible fungi to be found.

On Tuesday, I am informed by the boss who was *not* out of town after all, that Monday was the busiest in three years. He also informs me I am again unemployed. Bosses, it seems, are cursed with neither subsistence genes nor compassion for employees who are.

And Here's Another Tip...

Recently, I have been perusing the back shelves of the county library, hoping to check out one of those "coffee table" books with the scenic covers and mammoth dimensions. Lacey's Aunt Bernie is flying in sometime this month from Minneapolis, and Lacey feels the dear lady will be upset to discover we have cracked the glass on the rattan coffee table she sent us for Christmas a couple years ago. She figured camouflage in the form of a big book would be just the ticket; we can cover the crack until Bernie leaves and the table goes back to the shed. Personally, I feel Aunt Bernie would be better off if she knew rattan furniture looks really dumb in a log house. Lacey tells me you can't say stuff like that to favorite relatives, however.

While shuffling through a shelf of large but tasteless medical volumes with illustrations of the human anatomy in various stages of deterioration, I discovered a misplaced edition of the 1984 Guinness Book of World Records, and without consciously making the decision to waste a half day, I was soon planted at a table devouring amazing statistics, fantastic records, and unbelievable columns of firsts, worsts, bests, and largests.

Mr. Walter Cavanagh of Santa Clara, California, I discovered, has the world's largest collection of valid credit cards—some 1,122 worth 1.25 million dollars in credit. On another page, I read that Joseph Hruby of Lyndhurst, Ohio, is the proud owner of 165,480 cigar bands dating from 1895. There were, of course, many other similarly exciting tidbits, but you can imagine my excitement when I discovered that I, too, might qualify as one of the elite members in this prestigious compilation of dumb things to save. Nowhere in the book was there mention of anyone with a more extensive collection of fishing rods with broken tips.

I began accumulating my impressive store of tip-less rods when, at age nine, the spokes of my Schwinn bike gobbled the last six inches of a two-piece glass rod with a wooden handle. To its credit, the rod put up a terrible fight, and when the dust settled, the bike and I both looked like we'd been mugged by a Pontiac. After the bleeding stopped, I stashed that rod under my bed because even at that age I couldn't bear to throw stuff away. It not only survived numerous moves and spring house cleanings, it soon began to attract broken-tipped kin, and before I knew it, I had a collection of 40.

That collection is still growing. It doesn't seem to matter anymore if I purchase rods made from fiberglass, boron, graphite, or bamboo. It doesn't seem to matter that these rods can be bent tip to butt, tied in a knot, or even used to catch fish; in less than a year, I will have reduced their lengths by at least three inches. I am the Hurricane Hugo of fishing rods.

If I leave a fishing rod in a car trunk longer than an hour, it will be broken when I take it out, and it matters not that the car sat in the driveway with no further human interaction. Screen doors are even worse. If I push through a screen door carrying an armful of firewood, it will bounce back and forth 15 times, letting the heat out and the dogs in. If I push against that door while carrying a fishing rod, however, it will immediately slam shut. Over half my broken rods are direct descendents of the union between a screen door and a door jamb. I cannot bear to give these bastard children to the garbage man as I know there just *has* to be a use for a tip-less fishing rod.

At one time, I thought I could eliminate my glut of useless broken-rods by taking up ice fishing. Ice fishing rods *should* be short. Mainly, one just needs something to attach the line to. Twenty-three ice fishing rods later, however, I suspected I had too many; I didn't even *like* ice fishing.

Next, I began hanging mangled rods like trophies from the walls of my den. I figured people would come over, view the carnage, and say, "Man, you've had on some whoppers!" Then, I could be modest, massage reality a bit, and feel good about myself. Feeling good about yourself is very important these days. It is particularly important if you have the social worth of a pine beetle and the personality of a cotton swab. Sadly for me, people caught on before long. They would glance at my newest broken rod and ask, "Front screen or back?"

I still refuse to believe there is no place in this world for broken-tipped fishing rods. I have used a few as tent stakes, a few more as carp spears, and several as curtain rods. Currently, I am experimenting with garden stakes, but it is driving me crazy to look out the kitchen window and see $480 worth of angling equipment holding up a half dozen scrawny tomato plants that will produce no more than two dollar's worth of fruit. At the rate I'm breaking rods, I'll have to enlarge the garden by three plants annually just to keep up. Heck, I don't even like tomatoes.

From the Desk of Alan Liere

Dear President Clinton:

When we were just little little guys, our mothers told us we would be president of this great country some day. Well sir, mine was wrong. Yours wasn't, though, and I want you to know there are no hard feelings.

I read in the paper, Mr. President, that you went duck hunting. I read, too, that you were only out a couple hours and that you didn't get to the blind until full daylight. I feel bad about that. I understand someone shot a duck, but the paper said no one was taking credit for it. Believe me, sir, you should have taken it home and asked Mrs. Clinton to stuff it. Hot roast duck is delicious.

While your "hunt" was a nifty piece of fence-walking, I am afraid it will take more than two hours in a marsh to alleviate American sportsmen's concerns regarding your numerous firearms proposals. You may think you're more evolved than I, sir, but that fiasco in the swamp was no closer to a duck hunt than is a golden delicious to a road apple. A real duck hunt begins months before the first frost. On a warm Saturday, you dump your decoys out on the back lawn. You wash off the mud with a garden hose, scrutinize each to determine which need new paint, and inspect the anchor cords. You take your time with the repairs, perhaps even stringing them out longer than necessary, for this is your livin' time, one of the things you can do each year that is guaranteed to make a difference. You let your retriever out of the kennel to supervise. She'll sniff around and slap your leg with her tail and watch you with absolute adoration and understanding as you go about your happy business, and you'll know you couldn't have done the job right without her. Ritual, Mr. President! Anticipation. That's duck hunting.

Now plan a wild game dinner with your relatives and friends. It doesn't have to be elaborate. More an excuse than anything. Clean out the freezer. Swap recipes. Tell your stories twice, show off your new goose call, make plans for October. Laugh. Joke.

A celebration of life, Mr. President. Kinship! Renewal! That's what it's all about.

A couple weeks before the opener, start making phone calls.

"Hey Dave—Is there any water in that pond out in the scab rock? What about the blind? Shall Eddie and I come down with some old plywood?"

"Is that son of yours still itching to do some duck hunting, Bill? Let's see if we can get him out this year."

"Sure, Mark—I can meet you the second week of the season. Bring that new pup you've been bragging on."

"Of course there's room for the kid, Bob. Glad to have 'em."

Tradition, Mr. President. Bonding. It's not just the shots.

On opening morning, get to the blind early with your Thermos. Wrap your hands around a steaming cup of coffee and hold it close to your face so the steam mixes with your breath. Watch the pinks and oranges gently unfold in the east and listen to the roar of silence. Soon, you'll hear wings in the darkness overhead and the dog will begin to whine and tug at her leash and a funny, shivery feeling that's part excitement and part something else will settle in your lower stomach and stay there until you rise to shoot. That's duck hunting, Mr. President. It's a process, don't you see? If you leave out a part, you don't get any of it. Even if a duck drops into your blind. Even if ten ducks drop into your blind. And it doesn't change from one end of the season to the other.

Like I said, sir, I feel bad for you because a duck hunt should start early. Oh sure, I know there's a lot of people telling you what to do and where to go and a lot more standing in line to do the same. I know the President of the United States of America thinks he has to please us all or he won't be re-elected and get to take all those neat trips to Camp David and Martha's Vineyard and Africa and such. But it must really get confusing sometimes when you have to keep pretending you're both for and against everything. Have you ever worn your PETA hat to a Ducks Unlimited fund raiser or cheered for the Yankees in Seattle? Have you ever thought about what these votes are costing you, President Clinton? One day this circus you've brought to town will be over, and when you go home, you'll have the time for a long look in a full-length mirror. Most likely, you still won't be a hunter, and that's all right. Your choice. But if you keep messing with the Second Amendment, I won't be a hunter, either. And that will be your choice, too. It just doesn't seem right.

Very sincerely yours,

Alan Liere

The Ultimate Snipe Hunt

Whenever outdoorsmen get together to overeat and reminisce, one of them will eventually be compelled to relate the details surrounding his adolescent snipe hunt. After sharing in these nostalgic assemblages more than three decades, I have decided I am the only youth never duped into holding the gunnysack at the end of the corn row, crouching expectantly at midnight, sack open, waiting for Uncles Dexter and Tiny to chase the creatures—whatever it was—toward me. The fact is, I didn't have an Uncle Dexter, and Tiny drank too much beer to be very creative at midnight. Fortunately, I did not suffer unduly for this omission during my developmental years, as my sister's first boyfriend, Bick, was a goose hunter.

My father did not view Bick Schuster with much affection. For one thing, Bick was a drummer in a fledgling rock band called The Real Toads, and for another, he didn't have a crew cut—reasons enough at the time to eye him suspiciously. Bick hoped he could shore up his unstable position in our family by pretending he liked *me*, who *did* have a crew cut, and for that reason, I was invited to go goose hunting with him. At 15, I was unaware the outing would doom me to a life of snipe hunts.

Bick and his cousin, Jack, picked me up at 3 a.m. on a snowy, minus-14 December morning. Their chosen hunting spot for this, my maiden venture, was the winter wheat country

150 miles southeast of town, and in Bick's ancient, heaterless coupe, it promised to be a long, cold drive. Fifty miles into our odyssey, Bick's vehicle quietly died. "It's the carburetor again," he announced, coasting to the shoulder and turning on the left blinker. "She's frozen." Ordering me from the car, he grinned. "Don't worry," he said, "the three of us can fix it."

Several minutes later a station wagon pulled alongside and stopped parallel to us on the highway. The dome light went on, and I squinted through the blackness as an elderly lady rolled down the passenger-side window. "Do you need. . . ." she started to ask, but then frantically cranked up the window, slammed the accelerator to the floor, and lurched off into the night. The sight of the three of us kneeling on the front fender of Bick's car as we urinated on a frozen carburetor had no doubt caused her to rethink her inclination to extend aid.

Miraculously to me, my embarrassment was not in vain. Though it doesn't smell so great for a few miles, warm urine will thaw a frozen carburetor, and we were soon on our way again. When we eventually overtook our almost-Good Samaritan, Bick pulled around and passed with a friendly honk. A short time later, though, the same lady came by again, this time treated to an even greater spectacle as we attempted to duplicate our previous miracle with empty bladders.

Eventually, we got around to the business of hunting geese. In what seemed to me a random act, Bick pulled over in the deep blackness. "We're here," he announced. "Jack and I will haul the decoys—you bring the guns, ammo, and sheets."

"Sheets?"

"Yeah, sheets," he mimicked. Then, remembering his ulterior motives for bringing his girlfriend's brother along, explained, "We lay in the snow with sheets over us. It works good."

I didn't even like the sound of it, but I kept quiet, did as I'd been told, and plodded behind Bick and Jack through eight inches of fluffy new snow. In the cold air, my runny nose formed unattractive, antique-white icicles above my lip.

At last, we were far enough, and I gratefully released my burden, removed my gloves, and attempted to ascertain the nature of the frozen digits attached to my palms.

"Don't just stand there looking pretty," Jack ordered sarcastically. "Let's get these decoys out."

Geese winged over us, a few singles venturing low for a better look even as we placed the silhouettes. When the task was complete, I laid down as directed, pulled a sheet over me, and winced as Bick kicked snow onto the covering. "You'll be fine," he said, as I was consumed by cold and claustrophobia.

Truly, a snipe hunt would have been more productive. Only once during the entire day was the numbing cold pushed momentarily into the closet of my consciousness. At three in the afternoon, six big Canadas appeared from nowhere, ten feet off the ground. Dissecting our spread, they made a large loop and returned, feet down, wings loudly lashing the air.

"Take 'em!" Bick yelled.

There was a frantic rustling, a flurry of shots, yelps of success. Sadly, none of them were mine. I was hopelessly encased in a white sheet, and like a moth emerging from a cocoon, I thrashed piteously, caring less about shooting a goose than in seeing one close up.

Once one has hunted geese, has heard the bewitching "ha-ronk" and experienced the power, speed, and elegance of flight, he can never again be the same. He'll see them in his dreams; he'll hear them in the shower. Shortly after that first goose hunt, my sister gave up Bick for a trombone player with good lips, and after I got my driver's license, my subsequent efforts became solo forays into snipe country.

Usually, I set up in the wrong field. Often, my fingers were too numb to release the safety. Sometimes, I was engaged in warm-up calisthenics when the birds appeared. Nothing will discourage a goose from landing like a man with his hands in his pants running in place in a winter wheat field.

My pursuit of wild geese was consuming and continual. Many years later, my persistence paid off and I dropped a honker in a field of harvested peas not too far from home. It took several more years before the feat was duplicated. I've worked out some bugs in technique in the decades since, but as often as not, I come home knowing I would have done as well with a gunnysack at the end of a corn row.

I'm Not Tired, I'm Happy

My cousin's husband, George Twigg, says nothing ages a bird hunter like youth—the one sitting next to you on the drive home.

Oh, he can still walk George Junior's legs off in a section of cut corn, and it will be a few years yet before the kid can double on pheasants. He'll be darned, he says, if he'll let a 15-year-old upstart with but three seasons under his oversized vest do all the brush work while he waits at the end of the draw, and when it comes to getting off a shot, he's still the fastest gun on the block.

It's those rides home that are aging him, he says. It's those cold, dark nights with the heater going full blast, when the snow is coming right at you no matter which direction you travel. It's the lulling highway song of studded retreads on black ice, the dog snoring in the back seat, and Waylon Jennings on the car radio.

I know just what George means, but I don't happen to think post-hunt drowsiness has anything whatsoever to do with getting old.

It used to be I could work all day, play all night, and still be there drinking black coffee at the kitchen table and ready to go when my hunting partner, pulling into the driveway, flashed his headlights across the back of the house. It used to be. Caffeine and anticipation would keep me wired no matter how long the drive, and my passion for hunting would not let me quit until I had taken a legal limit or the game was called on account of darkness. Even then, it was usually I who took over the driving duties for the trip back home, and I derived tremendous satisfaction in the knowledge I could do it all again the next day if I wanted. Many times I did.

Like my bald spot, my own post-hunt drowsiness kind of snuck up on me, and I didn't know I had it until it was there. It started about the time I decided there was no use getting to the pheasant draws before the birds had stretched and walked around a bit—more scent for the dog, you know. Then, the next season, I, who had never before enjoyed food with my coffee, woke up ravenous every Saturday morning, and it wasn't too difficult to convince my gunning chums that a short stack and a couple eggs would be a good way to start the morning. "Let's meet at the Denny's on Third Avenue—say eightish. We can still be on that side hill by 9:30."

I was also finding that though I could hunt all day if I had to, I never had to. It wasn't that limits were being taken any sooner; I just didn't need to shoot as often to have a good time. Sometimes I didn't shoot at all. I began to notice things, like the way a marsh hawk can hang motionless in a breeze, and how the smell of cottonwood lingers in your nostrils and sticks to your clothes long after you've worked through the stand and wandered into the stubble. In winter I studied animal tracks, and witnessed, second-hand, the violent dramas played out in fresh snow—weasel gets quail, owl gets weasel. So many things I'd been missing.

I nearly fell asleep following the dove opener this year. My son, Matt, and I decided to indulge in a hundred-mile, two-day outing before school started, and we drove through Colfax down to Penewawa on the Snake River. We could have hunted in our back yard, but I wanted to show Matt a place I'd gone as a kid, a gnarled peach orchard by an abandoned grain elevator where the doves flew over in uncountable waves after feeding across the river in the wheat. It was an easy hunt with quick limits both days, and there was no reason for me to be tired on the trip home.

"Dad," Matt said as I leaned forward on the steering wheel and stared at the hypnotic blur of the yellow line, "do you want me to drive?"

I'd forgotten, of course. He'd earned his driver's license in February. Sixteen years old. What had happened to 14 and 15? Hadn't he just learned to ride a bike?

Pride was overruled by good sense. Of course he should drive. I pulled over at the next wide spot on the highway and turned the task of delivering us safely home to my son.

"You gettin' old or somethin', Dad?" He grinned as he took the wheel.

"Not just yet," I replied, pulling the lever that made the seat lie back. "Crank the heater up a notch, will ya?"

"Are you really that tired?" he asked.

"Contented, my boy," I sighed. "Contented. Watch the road."

OH, Canada!

Normally, I fish in the summer and hunt in the winter. It's not that I'm opposed to being cold, but that I'm opposed to being cold in a boat. For that reason, trout fishing in February has always been way below both golf *and* tag team wrestling on my list of fun things to do with my clothes on, and ever since I gave up skiing because I'm allergic to pain, Canada has not been my winter dream destination. Nevertheless, on a recent winter weekend, two friends, Mike and Dale, enticed me with tales of giant Gerrard rainbow, into fishing across the border with them in British Columbia's Kootenay Lake.

We headed out late Friday afternoon, and early Friday evening I was sitting at the Nelway Border Crossing talking to a nice Canadian custom's inspector who very much wanted to put me in a nice Canadian jail. Custom's inspectors, it seems, do not have a sense of humor.

I don't know what made me give her a false name, I really don't. Mike and Dale, after all, had said *theirs* correctly. When she asked about my citizenship, I faithfully said, "U.S." When she asked my reason for visiting Canada, I truthfully said, "Fishing." When she asked my name, I said "Proctor Smith." When she asked for my I.D., I said, "Kings-X."

"My real name is Liere," I told her quickly. "Alan Liere. I'm a very nice person. It says so right here on my driver's license."

"How is it," she asked without smiling, "that you said 'Proctor Smith'?"

How indeed? To be honest, it had just struck me funny that

my two friends would answer with their correct names and I would not. I suppose I was thinking more about their reaction than hers, imagining them suppressing their giggles in the front seat while in the back seat, I pulled a harmless but immature fast one on the custom's inspector.

"I got confused," I finally said. "I thought I was in Miss Drivel's Algebra class. We never gave our correct names to the sub in Miss Drivel's Algebra class."

"I see," said the custom's inspector in a way that made it obvious she not only did *not* see, it wouldn't matter if she did. "Miss Drivel, eh?"

"That's right," I grinned hopefully. "Miss Drivel was hardly ever there; I think we made her nervous. We almost always had substitute teachers. I think we made *them* nervous, too. We thought it was pretty cool to try and confuse them. I guess maybe you reminded me a little bit of Mrs. Fish."

"Mrs. Fish, eh," said the custom's inspector. "And that would be whom?"

"Earlene Fish," I said nervously. "One of the substitutes. And," I continued hopefully, "one of the handsomest, most magnanimous women I knew. Mrs. Fish would sometimes let us eat corn nuts while we watched *Hemo the Magnificent*."

"You watched *Hemo the Magnificent* in Algebra?" the custom's inspector asked. "Isn't that about the heart?"

"Heck, we even watched *Hemo* in Pacific Northwest History," I said. "Whenever we had a substitute we watched *Hemo*. I saw it 23 times in junior high. I don't think they paid their subs very well."

The custom's inspector was shaking her head. "Now I'll have to look at *your* licenses, too," she said, addressing Mike and Dale. "Harboring a lunatic is serious business." With all three in hand, she then walked into the custom's building and disappeared from view.

"Proctor Smith?" Mike hissed. "Proctor Smith?" Dale didn't even turn around, but I could see his jaw working. Either he had taken a mighty big bite of beef jerky, or he was boiling mad.

I had pretty much slunk down as low as I could get in the back seat when the custom's inspector lady returned to the car 15 minutes later.

"You two can go," she said, handing licenses back to Mike and Dale. I whimpered. There was a long pause. "And I'm afraid you'll have to take this one with you," she added, handing me a license, also. The faintest suggestion of a smile cracked her face. "Make sure he takes his medicine. Good fishing, gentlemen."

The car roared to life and lurched forward. "She called me a gentleman," I said.

"She hasn't got to know you," Mike growled.

"She almost did," I said.

"Shut up," Dale suggested.

It seemed like a pretty good idea. He probably should have mentioned it earlier.

Shortcuts Ain't

It is 87 miles from MY PLACE to THAT PLACE; I can find the route on any state map. Logically, there is but one way to get there, but I have a friend who knows a shortcut. So do you. "It'll save a half hour," he'll tell us. "It winds through some of the most spectacular country you've ever seen." We want to believe. Maybe this time it will be different. Maybe this time he actually knows of what he speaks. We bite our lips. Our friend notices this and moves in with the kicker: "Don't forget what Robert Frost said about a road less traveled!"

I admire Robert Frost. He wrote some poetry I can understand. I seriously doubt, however, that the father of modern American poetry ever got lost trailering a boat down a deer trail on the advice of a friend. A "road less traveled" is one thing, but a shortcut is quite another. Shortcuts can last forever. My brother-in-law, Thayer the Abnormal, suggests my recalcitrance is due to a deficient pioneer-spirit chromosome. My ancestors, I remind him, suffered hardships mapping this great land, and it would be ungracious of me to let all that suffering go to waste. Besides, I do not see the correlation between pioneer spirit and driving an air conditioned 4x4 with power steering and cruise control to Wall Lake where I will consume three deli sandwiches, drink a six pack of diet soda, and release every fish I catch. I mean, this isn't exactly subsistence angling.

This is true, Thayer will tell me, but it is UN-AMERICAN to waste time and gas when a shortcut will save both. I wholeheartedly agree, I tell him, but it has been my experience that shortcuts save neither. The last time we took one of your shortcuts was the day we headed out for some crappie fishing at Bonny Lake and ended up in the middle of the Bare Buns Fun Run at the Kaniksu Ranch by Deer Lake where I had to take off my pants to ask directions.

Shortcuts ain't. Though my tenth-grade geometry teacher used to throw blackboard erasers at me in frustration, I left her tutelage with two axioms firmly ingrained: one was that the number of corn nuts I could consume in a 50-minute math class was directly proportionate to how close I sat to the teacher. The other was that the shortest distance between points A and B is a straight line, but only if a highway connects them. Plowing past point C, wandering over to point D, and climbing point E for a look around will not get you there sooner, easier, or more economically.

In the years since my high school incarceration, I have gathered many insights about life on the "outside." Never mind that I still cannot balance my check book, change the oil in the truck without damaging the transmission, or flip on a light switch without shouting "It's a miracle!" Never mind that I actually talk to phone solicitors, buy light bulbs by mail, and send cash contributions to societies for saving whales, banning nukes, and nuking whales: I know shortcuts and so should you. That they may be avoided, I have included here the five characteristics of shortcuts and the appropriate action to take when a fishing partner—the designated driver—insists on taking "a road less traveled."

> 1. A shortcut is always a road/path/trail/whatever on which the driver has either *never* been, or has not been in the previous 15 years. The last time he even passed through the area, he was on his way by airplane to Guatemala, but your presence in the vehicle has given him confidence to "try something different." Offer no encouragement! Immediately wrest the steering wheel from his grasp and bring the vehicle to a stop. Threaten to get out. Better yet, threaten to put *him* out.

2. A shortcut is often suggested when time is of the essence. This is the worst possible time. If you absolutely must be back in four hours and the driver says he can cut 20 minutes off the trip with a shortcut, it is even money you will not make your appointment that week. Emphatically explain your preference for the old, longer route, and bring out a road map to emphasize the logic of sticking to what you both know. Then, roll it up and smack him behind the ear.

3. If the road you are on becomes so dusty you cannot breathe and the driver is hitting ruts that loosen your fillings and send them careening off the cab windows like little pieces of shrapnel, you are taking a shortcut. Act quickly! The further you travel, the less likely your chances of ever having children. Feigning a seizure will usually get the car stopped long enough for you to "discover" you have left your pills at home. Suggest to the driver you return immediately to asphalt. If he is reluctant, a series of screeches, or a sudden, close-up, bug-eyed scrutiny of his belt buckle will get him moving in the right direction. A little drooling can't hurt, either.

4. Shortcuts never have road signs or any indication of human activity. If you *do* happen to spot a house way back in the brush, it will look distressingly similar to the mansion in Alfred Hitchcock's Psycho. Start whimpering. Hum the theme music to Jaws. Put your head out the window and roll it up on your neck. Scream for your mommy. Be creative. Your only concern is a U-turn.

5. If you find yourself wondering how anyone will ever find you again when the oil pan is ruptured, you are taking a shortcut. Cock your head, frown, and pretend to listen attentively to the engine/transmission/whatever. Say, "Sounds like you mighta thrown a fanning caster. Let's see if we can baby this hummer back to town." If the driver scoffs at your diagnosis, sneak your arm out the window

and furtively slap your palm against the door at irregular intervals. Eventually, poke your head out the window, look down toward the rear of the vehicle, and say "**Oh my gawd!**" Then repeat your diagnosis.

With these tips and insights you may possibly lessen the trauma of a shortcut and get in a lot more fishing time besides. A road less traveled may make all the difference, but Interstate 90 is quicker.

The Pffftt-Click Season

Opening Day, 1962.
Eddie Shawgo, Budd Woods, and I buried our faces in the weeds of a makeshift blind off Rock Lake and tried not to look at the geese circling the decoys. None of us had ever fired on a honker, and the excitement was almost unbearable.

After tantalizing us for nearly five minutes, a single bird cupped his wings and headed in. Then, the entire flock was settling, and on a signal from Budd, we stood, slapped shotguns to shoulders, and opened up. Pffftt. BANG! Click. Pop. The Pffftt-Click season had begun.

For his 17th birthday, my best friend, Eddie Shawgo, became the envy of a small group of 11th-grade boys when his grandmother gave him a shotgun-shell reloader. Somehow, he, I, and a few close friends had been temporarily spared the grief induced by run-away hormones, grappling only with one dilemma of consequence during our endless days in high school where to get the money for the shotgun shells we needed each weekend. Soon after acquiring his reloader, Eddie proclaimed our problems were over: if we would provide the hulls, he would reload them for us at cost.

I don't really think Eddie knew what he was getting himself into. The responsibility was monumental. There were only five months until the next hunting season began, and he was committed to reloading enough shells for himself and six friends who together could barely break a dozen clay pigeons in a day of marathon shooting. In his determined haste, Eddie spilled a lot during his early reloading activities. The lead shot from his initial session ruined his grandmother's vacuum cleaner, and the powder caused a flash-fire on her kitchen floor. Like grandmothers everywhere, however, the dear lady just ignored the scorched linoleum and retired to her sewing room with a bottle of Four Roses whiskey.

In late August, Shawgo reloads hit the market at $1.50 a box, and to our inexperienced eyes, they appeared to be reasonable facsimiles of "store-bought" loads. They were to be responsible for the preservation of more game birds than the combined efforts of Ducks Unlimited, The Audubon Society, and the State Department of Fish and Wildlife.

Back on Rock Lake, Eddie sloshed toward his downed goose, throwing up great, foamy sheets of water, his excited whoops filling the autumn air. A flock of wigeons wheeled directly overhead and a pair of teal zipped by at ten feet, but Budd's pump gun wouldn't pump, and I was frantically searching for a stick to push the swollen casing from the left breech of my double. Shawgo reloads.

Beginning that day, we learned that appearances were not all that indicative of a shotgun shell's ability to perform. "Pffftt," for example, meant Eddie had reloaded dry powder into damp casings. "Pffftt" followed by an evil smell meant he hadn't blown the debris from inside before adding powder, and "pffftt" or an anemic "pop" followed by a trickling sound meant that number four shot was rolling slowly down your barrel. A dull "click" meant that in his haste to meet his reloading obligations, Eddie had re-inserted a spent primer, and it mattered not if the sound was "pffftt, click," or "Bang!" if the casing was paper and had been lying around in a soggy duck blind for a season before Eddie reclaimed it; there was no way that shell was going to eject.

None of us had yet acquired much proficiency in the use of

a shotgun, but recollections of the past season made us certain our birds-taken-per-shots-fired ratio had surpassed both ludicrous and pathetic during the '61-'62 hunting season. It wasn't even the Shawgo reloads as much as what their unpredictability did to our nerves. The realization that our next shot might not result in the expected "BANG!" had a tendency to impair a swing already jerky with the exuberance and inexperience of youth.

The last hunt of the year followed on the heels of a late freeze. Despite numerous frustrations, I was, as usual, sorry to see the season ending. Eddie's reloads had definitely provided fodder for humorous reminiscing and made each bird taken more special. On January 12th, Budd, Eddie, and I lay in the snow beneath sheets and trembled as a flock of geese set their wings and glided into our decoys. We listened to the "whoosh" of wings as the magnificent fowl lowered their landing gear, and then Budd's "TAKE 'EM!" Throwing back our coverings, we sat up. "Pffftt. BANG! Click Pop." Eddie was up, tearing after his downed honker. The season ended as it had begun.

Bullhead Saturday

As cold and wet as it was, we should have stayed home, but uncluttered Saturdays are a rarity any more. And angling, I reminded my spouse in a rare burst of perception, is like watermelon and life in general; without the bad, you can't appreciate the good.

Following a few of the usual organizational mishaps, the trip shaped up nicely. The torrential rain had become a mere deluge, and in a few hours Lacey and I had filled a galvanized wash tub with water and three dozen Sprague Lake bullheads. On the drive home, I smugly reminded her that my foresight in including the washtub would assure we would not have to clean our catch immediately. Preparing these bewhiskered, prehistoric throwbacks for the table is not nearly as enjoyable as catching and eating them, and I can tolerate it much better if the task can be spread over a weekend. I was just about to declare it a royal flush day when, just north of home, a black plastic garbage bag I'd thrown in the bed of my truck to use as a rain coat caught the wind and opened like a parachute.

Through the rear view mirror I saw what was happening and I braked sharply, but the disaster was already in motion. Wrapping itself around my new, graphite-composition ultralight, the ballooning bag lifted the rod and reel into the air long enough for me to drive out from under them. When I finally braked to a stop on the narrow shoulder, I sat there staring helplessly into the side mirror as, reel-less now, the expensive rod flopped and squirmed on the asphalt under a continuous flow of traffic.

"Well, do something!" my wife said.

Forgetting the fish and the fact my pickup was without a tailgate, I whipped a U-turn. Immediately, some 36 bullheads and a galvanized wash tub of water slid out the back onto the yellow line. Lacey called my attention to this interesting development by shrieking my name several times.

Generally, I pride myself on my ability to remain calm when a good panic is in order, but the shrieking caused all my alarms to go off at once. My head was swiveling erratically from rear to side mirror, my pupils dilated, and I could feel a heavy sweat begin to suck my arm pits against my sides. Bullheads writhed on the wet asphalt while cars fishtailed to avoid them, horns blared, and windows full of teeth and pointing fingers blurred by. I flashed back to the day in my eighth summer when I accidentally propelled a golf ball through Mr. Kostelecky's 40-gallon aquarium and watched helplessly horrified as his tropical fish spilled out onto the living room carpet. "Let's get out of here!" I groaned, a vision of his murderous eyes glaring at me from the side mirror.

Fortunately, Lacey kept her cool. "Don't you dare leave those poor fish flopping out there in the highway," she hissed.

Ten minutes later, following many angry honks, squealing tires, and unintelligible taunts, the fish that had not become chowder were back in the wash tub. I retrieved my mangled rod and had almost made it back to the truck when my brother-in-law, Thayer the Abnormal, passed, laid on his horn, and pulled over. Thayer is not the type of individual to drive by a good disaster.

"How's the fishin', brother-in-law?" he smirked, eyeing the flattened bullheads I had kicked to the shoulder of the highway. His simpering smile spread over his face like warm, rancid butter as he delighted in my embarrassment. Then, he noticed the floppy, fractured fishing rod I held. "Whadja bring the jump rope for?" he asked.

Foolishly, I expected sympathy. "It's my new ultralight, Thayer," I whined. "It fell out of the truck."

"Looks like it mighta affected the action a bit," Thayer chuckled. "'Course, I don't know the requirements for this here asphalt fishin'." He looked at me and shook his head slowly. "Don't know 'bout you neither, brother-in-law," he said. "Seems Sis coulda done better."

When we got home, Lacey immediately ran the hose into the tub while I apologized to and fussed with the finny survivors. "Lacey," I said, "let's fillet these things in the morning. I don't think I can face them again today."

My wife agreed. We transferred our catch to the wheelbarrow which had twice the capacity of the wash tub, filled it with water, and went inside to clean up.

After dinner, we went out to check on the fish and found several had given up the ghost. Lacey poked at one doing a feeble back stroke. "I don't think they're getting enough oxygen," she said. "They've got to be dealt with right now."

"Do you suppose Art would want some?" I asked. "He sure enjoyed the package of fillets we gave him last fall."

Lacey poked some more at another of the survivors and clucked sympathetically. "Why don't you run some over and see?" she said. "If he'll agree to clean half, we can do the other half tonight."

Rather than transfer part of the catch to another container, I set off across the lawn with the wheelbarrow, taking a short cut through neighbor Durwood's back yard. I had just pushed past his deck when the slider opened and he stepped out.

Durwood looked down at me without expression. "Taking your fishies for a ride, neighbor?" he asked.

"Durwood, I. . . . I. . . ." There didn't seem to be an appropriate response.

"No need to explain, neighbor," he said indulgently. "It's good to get 'em out on an evening like this—expand their horizons—let 'em see how the other half lives."

An hour later, Lacey and I and Norm Atchison stood on the bank of Norm's farm pond and waved goodbye to the bullhead survivors. Norm had graciously consented to the release.

"Seems like a waste of some good eating," he mused as the

disoriented fish swam about in short circles in the shallows before heading for deeper water.

"They earned it," I said.

On the way home, Lacey asked me if the day's events had been part of the good or the bad. I have no idea what she was talking about.

A Sign For Pease Mountain

For some time now, residents of other states (I call them exotics) have been awakening to the possibility there may be more to life than commuting to work on an interstate at 12 mph while being assaulted by someone else's cacophonic excuse for music and sucking in air that defoliates trees. Unfortunately, this enlightenment has resulted in an invasion of these parts.

Personally, I have no desire to cultivate additional neighbors, and these past few years have felt the need to buffer myself even further against exotic encroachment. That is why I bought 22 country acres behind Pease Mountain.

Local real estate agents tell me everyone is looking for the same kind of land; they want 10-25 partially-timbered acres with a view, a southern exposure, a good well, a year-round creek, and plenty of wildlife. Furthermore, it must be easily accessible—exactly the kind of place I found on Wildrose Prairie. My heirs, of course, will probably be paying for my acreage here long after I've sloshed across the River Styx—and they'll probably need *two* jobs just to pay the taxes. Right now I'm certain this place was a reasonably poor investment if I measure its value only in dollars and cents.

But what the heck. I've been a hunter for 35 years, and God willing, I'll still be one 35 years down the road; I thought it time I put something back. The idea of planting some cover and creating a wildlife refuge here pleases me mightily.

In my hikes around the property I have seen quail, pheasant, ruffed grouse, and deer. Mallards rest in the duckweed-covered pools, and doves fly in early and late to water. Last spring, I saw a cougar pad silently along the back fence line, and one wondrous summer morning, a trio of moose were nibbling willow shoots just off the road. With a little help, I think this could be a real nice parcel for all of them to loaf around unharassed, discussing the pond weed on the neighbor's half section and evaluating the aspen buds down where the spring runs into the creek. Sort of a retirement home for critters.

My new status as a land baron has also caused me some anxiety. For years, my hunting partners and I cursed, grumbled about, and felt persecuted by the presence of "NO TRESPASSING" signs. What right, we wondered, did one man's real estate contract have to deny us the privilege of hunting? Did he own the birds that inhabited his fence rows and wheat fields? Wasn't this America where one need not be rich, powerful, or in possession of good genes to go afield to recreate?

I'm happy to say my opinions about "rights" are better considered now than they used to be, and I have conceded to a land owner's prerogative to do what he darn well pleases with his own property as long as the E.P.A., the B.L.M., the Departments of Ecology, Health, and Agriculture, the Noxious Weed Board, the Aquifer Protection Agency, and the Paralytic Shellfish Poison Center agree with what he has in mind.

"NO TRESPASSING" signs still make me wince, but I understand, now more than ever. If I'm going to the trouble to plant habitat strips along Houston Creek, I sure don't want someone down there disturbing the animals when they're trying to eat or get a poker game going. Surely, though, there is a kinder, gentler way of indicating my desires than posting a glaring, orange and black sign that to me always said, "I do not know you, but you are probably a toad and I do not want you breathing on my property."

I have encountered a diversity of such signs in my years afield. The one I liked least, near Colfax, Washington, said

"Trespassers Will Be Violated." The ones I liked best was near a very rural farmhouse close to Rathrdrum, Idaho. It was green and black and said simply, "GO AWAY!" I have often wondered if the individual who put it up was anti-everything, or whether he was one of those pathetic individuals like myself who cannot say NO to small, runny-nosed children with something to sell.

The sign that made me run the fastest the other direction was near Medford, Oregon, at the bottom of what looked like a really great grouse draw. "BE A TUPPERWARE HOSTESS," it said. If I can't do better than that on Pease Mountain, I'll copy my Uncle Alvin who fenced his land and put a bison in the enclosure. When you've got a 2000-pound animal guarding the premises, you don't need a sign.

Until I Married Lacey

Until I married Lacey, I *always* had dry cereal, coffee, and orange juice for breakfast, I always had peanut butter and mayonnaise sandwiches for lunch, and I always had some kind of meat with potatoes for dinner. Until I married Lacey, my lunches varied only when I went hunting or fishing, and only then because they were carried afield in a bag and a thermos and consumed by nine a.m. rather than noon.

Lacey brought dietary diversity to our marriage. The trunk of my wife's family tree grew out of the big lake country of Depression-era northern Minnesota, but the roots extended all the way to Germany, and the branches had dropped fruit from Texas to eastern Washington. Meals in Lacey's family were a diverse accumulation of cultures and socio-economic alignments. Indeed, Old Country "dab of this, pinch of that" merged with Betty Crocker and New Country availability to create gastronomical adventures.

When I first met Lacey's parents, a stroll to the kitchen for a glass of water put me instantly on alert: there were *chicken feet* just barely protruding from a steaming kettle on the stove. My immediate impression was of awe. "You gotta see this," I told Lacey when I was back in the living room. "There's a couple chickens doing head stands in a kettle of boiling water on the stove."

Lacey followed me to the kitchen. "That's swartzsauer," she explained.

"Well, did you know there were chickens messing around in it?" I continued, nodding toward the stove. "And I think they might have drowned."

"It's swartzsauer," Lacey repeated. "My father makes it. There's *supposed* to be chicken feet in it. Duck feet, too, when we have 'em."

"What does he do with it?" I sniffed. "The toenails are still on."

"You don't eat the toenails, silly," Lacey laughed.

"I don't eat bird feet at all," I laughed back. "Especially chicken feet. All the chickens I know are very careless about where they walk."

"There's head meat, too," Lacey said proudly. "We don't waste a morsel around here. Goes back to the Depression, I guess." She picked up a wooden spoon, jammed it down between the protruding feet, and with one deft stroke, sent the whole mess swirling counter-clockwise. "You'd be surprised how much meat is on a chicken's head," she said, smiling pleasantly. "Feet, too. It will be ready in a few minutes."

"Head and feet meat?" The dark-colored concoction was still revolving slowly in the kettle—slower, I thought, than my stomach. I couldn't even assimilate the concept of swartzsauer. Eating it was out of the question.

Despite my coddled taste buds and lack of finances, Lacey eventually married me. Like most newlyweds, we thought we could live on the fruits of love, and like most newlyweds, it didn't take long to decide the fruits of love, though nourishing to the soul, do darn little to appease a growling stomach. The fact is, on an empty stomach, it is darn difficult to appreciate other delights. Fortunately, hunting season came along just in time, and we were blessed with a bumper crop of pheasants.

The first time I brought home a limit of roosters, Lacey fried one immediately and we ate prodigiously. The next day, we had homemade pheasant-noodle soup, and once again, we ate until our stomachs bulged. The third day, Lacey made a thin, tart pheasant gravy and served it over rice. It was dark and delicious, containing prunes and raisins and apricots and lots of little bits of meat.

"This is wonderful!" I enthused, dishing up a third helping. "Is this still part of those first three pheasants? "You sure know how to stretch a soup bone." It was a compliment I'd heard her father give her mother.

Lacey looked at me curiously from across the table. "Three pheasants?" she questioned. "We've been eating on the same bird for three days."

"Come on!" I exclaimed. "We ate a whole one the first day."

"Yeah, and the next day I made soup from the bones."

"No kidding!" I said. I studied my gravy. "But then where did all this extra meat come from?"

Lacey ladled out another portion for herself. Then she began poking at it with her spoon. "Well—here's some neck meat," she said, sorting through the gravy. "Here's some gizzard and a piece of heart." "And here," she said, putting her hand over her mouth and seeming to clear her throat, "is some hedinfeemeet."

"Hedinfeemeet?" I questioned. "Hedinfeemeet?" A long-dormant queasiness sprinted from my stomach and commenced to play squat-tag in my esophagus. "Head and feet meat? I'm eating pheasant head and feet meat? Lacey, I. . . ."

"Swartzsauer," Lacey corrected, "And you can't tell me you don't like it. Just watch out for the toenails."

From the Desk of
Alan Liere

Dear Donald:

It took me two and a half years to get a year of college under my belt, and here you've done it in half the time. I'm proud of you, nephew! Must feel pretty good.

The fact is, son, I didn't get too terribly serious about college until my father quit paying for it, and even then, I found higher education distracting. I wasted a lot of money and a handful of years. Seems like every time I turned around there was a paper or a book or a class trying to interrupt my irresponsibility, and I would have none of it! I think I told you I lived in a 12-story dorm overlooking a section of wheat stubble surrounded by scabrock ponds, and that certainly didn't help my concentration any, but I must admit the Goody twins—Angel and Devine—were as distracting as my penchant for duck hunting. I was an 18-year-old freshman with a major in English and minors in Pinochle and sleeping in; they were sixth-year seniors majoring in minors. I used to think I was pretty special to the Goody sisters, and if you don't count the football or baseball teams, I guess I was for a time. Like others before them and others since, however, they snuck off in the night with my Magic Markers.

Incidentally, your mom tells me you have a girlfriend, Donald. She also tells me you came home nearly every weekend to hunt ducks. I don't know how you swung that, but I'm glad to hear you still have your priorities in order. Like I once told you, son—"Girls don't migrate."

We've got a new dog, and I must say we are a lot more tickled about it than the neighbors were. Sadie is half golden retriever (theirs) and half black Lab (ours). Should be a fairly decent duck dog, don't you think? She has already begun to mellow out, so I doubt she will topple her father's chewing records. She's taken the corners off all the porch chairs and mangled a couple garden hoses, but her dad ate the porch itself and then devoured the sprinkler system, right down to the timer on the wall.

Last weekend, Sadie made her first live retrieve—not bad for 16 weeks of age! Lacey doesn't think the laying hen is going to pull through, but I am optimistic as it still had over half its feathers when we rescued it from under the porch. Of course, I feel terrible for the chicken, but you can't discipline a pup for something like that, can you? It reminded me of Old Ed's pointer. For two years the darn thing wouldn't retrieve anything, and then one day he brings home a peacock. Old Ed didn't know whether to beat the dog or buy it a steak. Anyway, that's three chickens in the last three years for us—one for each dog.

You asked about Goozer in your last letter. No, he didn't come back. Now there was an odd experience! I'm enclosing a picture Lacey took of us in Elwood Sloan's driveway. (Goozer is the one with the webbed feet). You can see why his sudden departure was not an entirely unwelcomed event in the neighborhood; that green cast on the cement slab in front of Elwood's garage is one day's accumulation of Canada goose effluvium. I have no idea why that bird landed in my back yard rather than on the lake, no idea why he stayed that week, and no idea why he left. I do know that grass passes through a goose faster than water through a hose, and that if goose residue is allowed to dry, it etches cement. Lacey asked Elwood if he would have any difficulty shooting geese this fall, knowing one of them could be Goozer. Elwood reminded her he didn't hunt, but after making the acquaintance of Goozer, he had been thinking about buying a shotgun.

Eat your heart out, nephew—I finally shot a canvasback! In fact, I shot a pair right out of your favorite blind on Winchester Wasteway. I took Bob down there on our annual December Disaster, and though we got the motor running this time, there was barely enough water in the channel to float a boat. It turned out Bob had forgotten his boots again, and I had forgotten my lunch, so we affected a trade of sorts and I pulled him through two miles of shallows in exchange for a sandwich which somehow evolved in those two miles from the promised rare prime rib with horseradish to stale peanut butter with grape jelly. Bob still insists he is mystified by the metamorphosis.

Anyway, the canvasbacks were the first I have taken in 35 years of duck hunting, so don't get to feeling too envious—I think I earned them. I always read about "cans" when I was a kid—authors like Nash Buckingham and Gordon MacQuarrie—but we just didn't have many in this flyway. This past season, though, everything came through. I even took a ringneck and a redhead—birds I hadn't shot since the '60s when I was too young to appreciate my good fortune. So guess what, kid? I now have a pair of mounted canvasbacks, a ringneck, and a redhead—in addition to the other dozen or so. I told Lacey we'd probably have to get rid of some furniture to make room for all the mounts. She suggested my easy chair and my liquor cabinet. Now tell me, young scholar, does that make any sense to you?

Keep up the good work,

Uncle Alan

Just Like In The Movies

Always a people person, Lacey has nevertheless accepted her husband's primeval need for reclusive weekend escapes. She not only tolerates this affliction, she sometimes encourages it by pitching in afterward to help me clean a mess of perch or pluck a brace of geese. She does this unselfishly and without undue malice, seldom extracting from me more than a promise to run interference for her at *Lamont's* annual red-tag sale.

Occasionally, usually after taking a *Reader's Digest* quiz to determine if our marriage is sound, I will agree to play Bingo with Lacey on Thursday night or catch a concert at the Arena, two activities I find only slightly more interesting than riding an exercise bike in the living room. She, in turn, will accompany me on one of my outdoor expeditions. Lacey has shivered with me in a duck blind on Winchester Wasteway, swatted mosquitoes with me from a canoe in Minto Flats, and groveled with me in the mud at Clam Gulch, Alaska. Because her sacrifices to preserving our marriage seem greater than my own, I am always looking for new outdoor pursuits she might actually enjoy. That's why I suggested mountain climbing.

We had just finished up a wet week in Alaska's Denali National Park where, inspired by the magnificence of North America's highest peak, I had decided to add crampons and an ice axe to my sporting accumulations.

"You know, dear," I said a few days after arriving back

home, "I've been thinking maybe we should try a little mountain climbing next summer."

Lacey froze in a stoop where she had been trying to remove her tennis shoes, halfway between the kitchen sink and the butcher block. I watched her shoulders rise as she attempted to suck all the air from the room in one gulp. Without turning or rising, she began to moan.

"On the other hand, dear," I said nervously, "I've wondered if perhaps *I* shouldn't try some mountain climbing next summer."

The air went out of Lacey's lungs in a great whoosh. "That would be different," she said calmly, "but can you afford it?"

"Well," I smiled with renewed confidence, "I don't think it would really be all that much. A guy at Denali told me good boots, an ice axe, and a pack would only run about $300. I figured that . . . ."

Lacey turned to face me. "Those aren't the expenses I was thinking about," she said slowly, pausing between each word.

"Well what, then?" I asked. "Once I've got some of the basic gear. . . ."

"Those aren't the expenses I was thinking about," she repeated. "Sure, you'll start out cheap—a sprain here, a laceration and some contusions there. Then you'll work up to broken legs and ruptured spleens, and the next thing I know I'll be hiring a helicopter again to look for you."

Oh come on, Lacey," I complained, "it's not as if I'm a total stranger to mountain climbing. Don't you remember when I participated in the Mt. Marathon Race a couple years ago up there in Alaska?"

"Yes," said Lacey. "I remember watching the first hundred finishers. I remember worrying about where you were. I remember thinking the search was going to be expensive. Alan—I walked all the way to the top looking for you before you got to the bottom. And that was just a hill. Calling Marathon a mountain is like calling that black, four-legged degenerate you keep in the kennel a hunting dog."

"Now hold on there, Sweetie," I said. "Let's leave Dude out

of this. It's true he has a few quirks and occasionally commits a social indiscretion at your pinochle parties, but he's just a pup."

Lacey was smiling, but I was pretty sure it wasn't sincere. "He's three years old," she countered. "He was expelled from obedience school, he's frustrated two professional trainers, and he's in a constant state of lust." The smile widened. "Hey—maybe you could take Dudie with you when you go play mountaineer. He could carry the bandages and splints."

"Well maybe I will," I blustered. It was so unlike Lacey to put a damper on my fun. "Maybe Dude and I will do just that." Turning, I strode from the room, cracking my knee on a chair. I tried not to limp too noticeably as I headed for the kennel.

"Dudie, 'ol boy," I said, scratching my black Lab behind the ear, "let's walk. Daddy needs to sort some things out." I knew a place less than a half mile from the house where a series of basalt monoliths jutted up like a row of knuckles from the edge of a cedar grove. It was a peaceful spot, a good place to cool off. Perhaps I'd even climb one of those rocks—check out some slightly rusted body parts and get a feel for my new sport.

Dude had a good romp on the way, but he stopped, whined, and lay down when I tried to coax him up the gradual incline at the base of the largest rock. Leaving him with the usually-unheeded command to "Stay," I scrambled easily on all fours toward the top, a mere 60 feet above me, and when I stopped to look down, he was still there. The rock steepened some at this point and I had to pick my route more carefully, but my confidence was high, the adrenalin was pumping double shots, and I moved smoothly upward. Helicopter, indeed, I thought.

With ten feet to go, my progress had slowed considerably and I was desperately looking for hand holds in the basalt. Then, I slipped and my right leg shot out into nothingness—a sensation I did not much care for but could not disregard. A nibbling fear crept beneath my cap to chew gently on my subconscious. It was very uncomfortable. A second time, a few feet further, my foot again failed to retain contact with the rock, and the nibbling became a hard chomp. Suddenly, I was remembering. It had been a long, long time, but I was remembering.

As a baby, I got nose bleeds in my high chair. Too much altitude. Then, at 20 months, I had suffered an unrestrained fall from my potty chair that set my toilet training back 15 years. For over 40 years, I had subconsciously avoided ladders and two-story houses. I even stayed away from potty chairs. Alone now on this treacherous, sheer rock, it had all come back. My brain dropped into compound low, my limbs ceased to function, and my eyes started to water. Fifty-five feet above the terra firma, I clung like a grease stain to the unfriendly slab and began to drip. I was in desperate need of some heroics, and I knew they wouldn't be mine.

"D-D-Dude," I called softly, afraid the sound would dislodge me, "g-g-go g-get M-M-Mom." Dude looked up at me and slowy wagged his tail. "D-D-Dude," I repeated tremulously, "wh-wh-where's your b-b-ball? F-F-Find y-y-your b-b-ball, b-boy." He yawned and put his head on his paws. "D-D-Dude," I hissed in final desperation, "h-h-h-hamburger. Wh-where's the h-h-hamburger?" Dude galloped around in an animated circle, his tongue flapping from his grinning jaws. Then he put his front paws on the rock and eyed me sympathetically. "F-F-Find the h-hamburger," I said, and I knew he understood what I wanted. With a single bark, he turned toward home. Just like the movies. Go, Lassie! Yo, Rin-tin-tin! Home, Buck, you wonder dog!

Five hours later, I limped through the dark into the kitchen. With some luck, Lacey would be asleep, as I needed several hours and a couple rolls of tape to reconstruct my frazzled libido and flayed epidermis. Wonder dog had been a no-show, and while I would have welcomed assistance in any form while clinging to that rock face, there was no way I wanted Lacey to know what had happened as long as I had gotten down by myself. Actually, once gravity had taken over, it hadn't been all that difficult.

"Are you all right, dear?" Lacey called from the bedroom. "I've been worried about you."

"Yeah, I'm fine," I lied, hurrying toward the bathroom. "Dude ran off and I've been looking all over for him."

"I just put him in the kennel," Lacey said. "He came home way before dark, ate, and sprawled out on the back porch for a nap." There was a lengthy pause. "Dear?" she called again.

"What?"

"Are you still upset?"

"Not at you."

"Are you coming to bed?"

"I'll be there in a bit, Lacey," I called. "As soon as I kick the dog good night."

Christmas Eve Day

    A pheasant hunt on the morning of Christmas Eve has been a personal tradition for many years. It began as a compensation for the inevitability of eventually facing 400 non-hunting relatives in a house with one bathroom and two chairs. In those dead, dragging hours before the package-opening frenzy commenced, I knew I would be obligated to kiss every aunt and explain to every uncle and second-cousin-twice-removed how it was I had attained the age of 19 without having a steady girlfriend, a decent haircut, or an intelligent answer to the question, "What are you going to be?" If I could go hunting first, I could tolerate it.
    Eventually, as I became more confident in who I was and what I stood for, a Christmas Eve morning hunt became a simple, foolproof way of monitoring myself and assuring I too, had participated in the loathsome shopping ordeal; if I hadn't purchased and wrapped all gifts by the 23rd, I couldn't go hunting on the 24th. A wonderful incentive.
    In those years and many that followed, I drove miles to do my pheasant hunting, but this year, I decided to try a little closer to home. There is a long, narrow draw on Wildrose Prairie just a few miles from home, choked with cattails and bordered by wild hawthorn. A small spring creek winds through it, and on many mornings I had seen iridescent roosters standing beneath the big cottonwood tree just off the road. The night before I wanted to hunt, I called the landowner, and at eight a.m. on Christmas Eve morning, my dog Sadie, and I drove slowly down the long driveway to his house, peering

expectantly beneath the Russian olive lining the way, the dog's magic, wet nose smearing the passenger-side window. We saw two pheasant roosters and four hens scratching for seeds in the wheat grass, and I felt good, convinced as always that spotting birds on the way in is a harbinger of good fortune. Though I had no intention of uncasing the shotgun until I had touched bases with the landowner, I would hunt more confidently knowing game was in the immediate area.

Sadie beat me up the steps to the porch, and then sat outside whining impatiently as I completed the formalities inside. It took a little longer than I had anticipated, but there was fruitcake and hot coffee, and I've never been able to turn down the opportunity to solve the world's problems in a warm farm kitchen.

After nearly a half hour, I returned to the truck, retrieved my old 12-gauge from behind the seat, and followed the bounding dog across the crusted alfalfa toward where the little creek dissected the property. In the corner of the field, near a crumbling, metal-wheeled hay wagon with wooden spokes, Sadie got hot, coursing frantically through a stand of head-high cane, streaking past a lone willow, and disappearing into a clump of wild rose and blackcap raspberry. She emerged, nose to the ground, tail flailing, and I tried to keep up. At one time, I called this process "running with the dog," but the last few years, I've called it "flirting with the big one." Cardiac arrest. Some of my friends have lost a step or two since their youth; I've lost the entire staircase.

Despite her enthusiasm, Sadie did not put a bird to wing. There was no bronze-tinged explosion—that wonderful, raucous, intimidating flush every pheasant hunter both anticipates and fears. Eventually satisfied her quarry had departed, she slowed ever-so-slightly and began to quarter.

On the sidehill above the draw where the wild hawthorn grows, a small covey of quail flushed wild and flew over the top. Sadie followed, flushing them again, but I was out of breath and could only watch. On the way back, she jumped a long-tailed rooster which tantalized me by flying almost close enough before veering off and sailing out of sight. After that, we hunted slowly toward a distant wood lot, rousting several hen pheasants and someone's black and white cat.

Finding no birds in the cattails, Sadie and I hunted one of the many finger draws leading up into the wheat stubble on top. Twice she became birdy, and twice I chugged along behind her, running on promise and instinct and nothing more, relieved I was not required to shoot. In the stubble, a small flock of Hungarian partridge, rare in this area, outsmarted us both, doubling behind before taking wing and sailing back down to the cattails we had just hunted. We followed the contours around and down to the wood lot on the far north end of the ranch, and there watched dejectedly as what seemed like every pheasant in the county flushed wild from a 20 x 20 foot patch of wild rose.

We turned back, trying not to retrace our steps, trying to cover fresh ground. Then, we were in sight of the farm house and my pickup, and I could almost smell the coffee. Only a quarter mile to go. Time to leave. You don't want to be late for Christmas Eve. Under a full head of steam, Sadie braked suddenly and turned sharply into a patch of tobacco weed. I pushed the shotgun's safety forward one more time. Two roosters, old and black and with enough tail feathers for a flock, exploded in a shower of ice crystals and seeds. The 12-gauge swung smoothly, seeming to calculate the lead on its own. Nothing left but to pull the trigger. At that moment, after six hours of hard hunting, I discovered I had never loaded my gun.

Those Birds In Thurmond's Garage

One of my best neighbors, Thurmond Walton, is a good man who would have probably made a decent county commissioner. Though he marches through life stepping high, Thurmond is never encumbered by the formality of a plan. He knows not where he is going, when he will get there, what he will do when he does, or why he would even want to.

A good insight into Thurmond's mentality is the "garage" he built for the family car. In the first place, it took him three years to complete because the project was inspired by a few pieces of scrap plywood he found in the vacant lot next door and decided to "use for something." During its various phases, the structure looked like a fish smoker, then a rabbit hutch, and then a McDonald's with a single arch.

Even when completed, the assemblage of wood, tin, tile, and brick had an identity crisis. Inside, it was a laundry room, a shop, and a walk-in closet for sporting goods. On the far side stood an upright freezer. Under the window were three bags of goose decoys suffocating under the weight of camouflage netting, a deflated three-man raft, extra garden hose, and some battered patio furniture. Beside that lay tackle boxes, reels, roller skates, and winter retreads, and the corners were crammed with boxes of Christmas ornaments and "good stuff" from Thurmond's six-year hitch in the Army. Everything but a car.

After lunch one afternoon, I walked over to Thurmond's house, hoping to borrow the electric hedge clippers I'd loaned him two months previously. Thurmond was busy in the kitchen feeding the waterdogs he was raising in the kitchen sink, and when he saw me heading for the garage, he came out on the porch.

"You might need some help in there," he said.

"Oh, I think I'll find what I need eventually," I joked. "Lacey doesn't expect me back 'til dinner time."

Thurmond jumped off the porch and intercepted me at the door to his garage. "There's something I need to tell you," he said mysteriously.

"Yeah?"

"Yeah. I should have told you a long time ago, but I wanted to surprise you and I thought it would be ready way before this."

I was intrigued. "A surprise for me? Now don't tell me—you finally found the lawn mower I loaned you last year."

Thurmond shook his head.

"The metric wrenches?" I asked hopefully.

"They're in there," he said. "I just can't get at 'em."

"Well, what then? What's the surprise?"

Thurmond grasped the door knob and tugged at the door. It stuck, then flew open in a cloud of dust and feathers. "It's turkeys," he said as a fine, white cloud settled over him. "I'm raising wild turkeys."

Thurmond Walton was, indeed, raising wild turkeys in his garage. Tottering on the rafters above, their red-wrinkled heads peering down at him as they pitched forward and back, two mature toms gobbled a welcome. Everything in the garage was encrusted in a whitish-gray blanket of droppings. "Probably could use a good cleaning," Thurmond said as he followed my gaze.

"Oh, I don't know," I said. "I think they missed a couple spots over there by the artificial Christmas tree." I peered into the far corner. "That *is* flocking on that tree, isn't it?"

"Some of it," Thurmond said.

Despite the strong ammonia smell, I stepped further into the garage. The mess was even worse than I had observed from the door. At least 200 yards of monofilament fishing line was wound about the interior, criss-crossing the center like a giant spider's web. Both light bulbs on the ceiling and two panes in the small, four-paned window were shattered, and the freezer, washing machine, and dryer were covered to a depth of four inches with "night deposits."

"Geez, Thurmond," I said. "What does Selma think of all this? You'd need a shovel to open the washing machine."

Thurmond kicked at the dried mess on the floor, then jumped back quickly to avoid a fresher addition from the rafters. "Selma is stayin' with Gramma for a spell," he admitted. "She said she'd be back when the garage was clean and the waterdogs were out of the sink."

"That long, huh?" I clucked sympathetically. I was studying the rafters again. "Most people get canaries and parakeets," I observed. "What are you planning on doing with these birds, Thurmond? You can buy fresh turkey for a buck-quarter a pound."

Thurmond prodded a whitish-gray tackle box with his foot. "It wasn't the meat I was after," he said. "It's the feathers, don'tcha know? Those little brown secondary feathers on the wings—the ones you use to tie up those muddler flies you're so fond of. I know how expensive they are, and I figured I'd grow my own and surprise you with 'em."

"Well, that was awfully thoughtful of you, neighbor," I said, "and it looks to me like they're ready. When's the harvest?"

There was a lengthy silence. Thurmond swatted at one of the numerous flies circling our heads, and when he finally spoke, his hand was over his mouth and his words were barely audible. "I'm a-thinkin' I'll let 'em go," he said slowly. "I'm a-thinkin' I'll give 'em to the Game Department to release."

I was disappointed. I could have really used those feathers.

"How come, Thurmond," I asked. "Is it Selma?"

The calloused hands he usually kept locked in his back pocket when he was talking were out, gesticulating wildly. "No, Selma hasn't got anything to do with it," he said. "At least not more 'n half." He shoved one hand back into a pocket and tried to relax. "I can't kill 'em," he said. "When I bought 'em in April, they were just about ready, but I didn't get around to it, and by the time I did, Selma had named 'em Homer and Simon, and that rascal, Homer, had plucked out almost all of Simon's feathers. So," he continued, "I had to hang onto 'em while Simon got his feathers back."

"But this is July," I said. "He must have been ready before now. You probably could have done it a month ago."

Thurmond grimaced. "You ever try to hold down an ornery 20-pound turkey that was beatin' you to death with his wings while his partner was struttin' on your back? When I brought the choppin' block out and grabbed Homer by the legs, he lifted me right out of my shoes. You can see what happened to the window and light bulbs."

"So then what?" I asked, trying with difficulty to look sympathetic.

"Well, Durwood next door offered to burn down my garage or drop a grenade in the dryer vent. I don't think Durwood is very fond of Homer or Simon. Said I'd ruined Thanksgiving for him forever." Thurmond had both hands back in his pockets, but his eyes betrayed some tension. "That's when I tried to snare old Simon with my snake-gitter, but when I looped that noose over his head, he took off through my fishin' tackle and pretty soon I was so wrapped up in mono I looked like a cocoon."

I was shaking my head in wonder, but Thurmond continued. "Then I snuck in here one night with a machete, and that," he said as he looked painfully toward a rack of mangled fly rods, "didn't work out very well, either."

"You should have asked for help," I said. "I used to butcher chickens every fall."

Thurmond walked under the rafters and looked up at

Homer and Simon. "Wanted to surprise you," he said. "Besides, it's too late now. I've promised 'em to the Wildlife boys. They said they'd give 'em some shots and turn 'em loose somewhere north of here." He glanced at me, shrugged, and ushered me from his garage without my hedge trimmers. "If those birds are as aggressive in the wild as they were here, we'll have a ton of gobblers in a couple years. And then, we can get those muddler feathers for the price of a turkey tag."

I'd Rather Be A Codger Than A Crank

A couple Saturdays ago, a bunch of us were sitting around Dale Ferguson's taxidermy shop, drinking coffee and watching Dale mount a Himalayan snow cock. One of his clients, a barber in Spokane, shot the giant chukar-like import last fall in Nevada, and though it was a first-year bird and not fully colored, it had not come easy; the barber was justifiably proud.

Before he was even halfway to the snow cock's domain, the man had sworn off pastry, sex, and tobacco and had scratched his Last Will and Testament on the face of his empty aluminum canteen. "Yeah," Dale commented, "he hunted three days and only took one bird, but he's an old codger and you gotta admire his grit."

It must be noted here that Dale Ferguson is a mere youth of 37 and hardly an authority on codgerdom. Nevertheless, I found it satisfying to note he used the correct terminology in describing the barber who, from all I've been told, truly is a codger. Though the word's origin is probably from the British "cadge," which means to sponge, peddle, or beg, an American codger does none of these things. Currently or formerly a hunter, he is over 65, respected if not loved by all, and most often in possession of several bird dogs, some long retired.

Not everyone can be a codger. Your cousin's neighbor,

I'd Rather Be A Codger Than A Crank   157

Didier Snodgrass, is a successful corporate attorney. He should be retired, but he's not. Didier is a dynamic, energetic individual. He has a Lambourgini, a townhouse, a young wife, and a stable full of polo ponies and polo pony residue. This is all fine and dandy, but at 71, Didier has never, ever been called a codger.

Didier's wife says he is a fuddy-duddy; his employees call him a geezer. His clients say he's a bit dotty, and the elevator man tells everyone the old boy is a crank. No one, though, will ever call Didier Snodgrass a codger because Didier Snodgrass possesses neither bird dogs, shotguns, nor acceptable state of mind. He never has.

Codgerdom is an acquired designation, a term of endearment reserved for a special kind of man. It calls forth visions of deep laugh lines, a special squint, rubicund cheeks, and a strong chin with short, white stubble. It smells like cottonwood trees, rose hips, and gun powder, and suggests independence and certainty and faith with perhaps just the faintest hint of crustiness.

To get there, a man has traversed hillsides, slogged through swamps, and followed narrow cow trails into thickets of wild plum. He has walked dozens of miles on railroad tracks, uncounted miles of logging road, and hundreds of miles of river bottom crop land. He's seen a red-tailed hawk pluck a cock pheasant off a fence post, watched a tom turkey stomp a five-foot bull snake, and been mesmerized by the courting dance of a sharptail grouse. Codgerdom, you see, is attained gradually during the journey rather than purchased at the end of the trip.

A codger can speak uninhibited English punctuated with the occasional profanity. He knows enough to save a good cuss word until it will do the most good. He knows, too, what is right and what is wrong, and he will not compromise an opinion for the sake of phony puritanical reticence.

A codger wears what pleases him. Put him in a pair of worn Levis, a briar-tattered flannel shirt with long johns showing at the neck, wool socks, and eight-inch leather boots with a little mud stuck in the cleats. Sit him down in an overstuffed chair in front of the fireplace and let a new litter of Lab pups chew on his fingers. The women will call him "sweet ol' thing."

There was a time not too long ago that I feared growing old, but somewhere in the last decade, I slipped quite comfortably, thank you, into advanced middle age. It ain't bad. I think codgerdom will be even better.

Grandpa's False Teeth

For the 15 years I knew him, Grandpa kept his false teeth in a front pocket. And though nothing the old man did after the nude flypaper incident in City Park really shocked us, we were mildly surprised he had paid good money for something he would try just once and put away. Grandpa, you see, was a thrifty sort, given to wearing pants until they disintegrated and boots until the soles became so slick he couldn't stand up. It must have distressed him something fierce to have those worthless, ill-fitting teeth, because he took them everywhere, presumably in the off chance they would get better with age.

As things turned out, neither the choppers nor Grandpa improved with age, but though in his later years he sometimes forgot a few details—like my name or where he left Grandma, he never, ever forgot those false teeth. Whenever he got tired of gumming peanuts or a piece of steak, Grandpa would threaten to put in "these gol-dang Roebuckers." Eventually, it became a family joke, and even today in my immediate family, worthless, non-functional objects are referred to as "Grandpa's false teeth." For me, many of these objects have to do with my outdoor pursuits. Chest waders, for example.

I purchased my first pair of chest waders from a local surplus store. "Slight irregulars," the salesman called them. That was many years before consumers developed even a modicum of shopping sophistication and everyone naively assumed the word "surplus" guaranteed a good buy. The thinking, of course, was that the price of an item "in surplus" was dictated by the law of supply and demand and that surplus goods would be sold in surplus stores at laughable prices. Sometimes, that was true. The problem, however, was that quality was also laughable. My first pair of chest waders kept my feet dry approximately 16 seconds, or until I had reached mid-stream. Thereupon, they quietly malfunctioned, allowing the waters of the Icicle River to enter, rise, explore, chill, and then anchor me solidly in place. It was at that time I began to suspect the primary function of waders was to prepare male occupants for a singing career with the Vienna Boys Choir.

With such a numbing start, one might assume those waders were discarded, but one would be incorrect. Even after I graduated from bicycle to Buick, I, like Grandpa, carried them around—under the seat of my car rather than my pocket—but with me nevertheless. Ten vehicles later, I still own those hip boots, taking them out occasionally to see if they are as miserable and non-functional as I remember. They are, but I can't throw them away.

Fingerless wool fishing gloves have also proven worthless to me. Fingerless wool fishing gloves keep only my palms warm—the parts of my hands that never get cold in the first place. When I first tried them on an ice fishing trip last winter, my fingers became so numb they wouldn't bend, and my friend, Mike, had to get the truck keys out of my jeans pocket for me at day's end. This caused quite a spectacle in the parking lot because the jeans were under my coveralls and a heavy blue parka was over that. Even so, it might have gone better had not Mike, also, been wearing fingerless wool fishing gloves.

The problem with those gloves was compounded by my reluctance to admit something so expensive could be so useless, and also by the fact I had seen a picture of some grim-faced men wearing the same gloves in an ice-fishing tournament. Now, a guy can pass up dinner now and then or even Friday night poker, but he never wants to pass up a chance to be grim; grim is macho. Grim suggests tolerance, even acceptance of pain. Never mind that those fishermen in the picture had recently shattered their frozen fingertips trying to slap their hands together for increased circulation. I could relate to them perfectly, and did in fact wear my fingerless gloves until I met a lady at a bass fishing tournament in New York who nearly laughed herself silly when I donned what she called "those worthless hobo mittens." Now, they have joined the chest waders under the car seat.

Also under the car seat is something most people have, talk about, and don't use intelligently. No, I am not talking about reproductive organs; I am talking about a compass. Any fool realizes you should never boat on large, unfamiliar water without a compass. A few also realize compasses do no good if you don't know how to read them. A friend of mine, Lardy James, didn't take this into consideration three winters ago, setting off alone on Destruction Bay for some winter whitefish angling.

When Lardy got back two years later, his wife was living with the dog catcher. Had my friend known how to work the compass he carried, this would have never happened, for Lena James was a wonderful woman and a devoted wife. When her man didn't return that winter or the next, however, she just naturally assumed he wasn't coming home. Responding to some normal, instinctive female urgings to have someone around to take out the garbage, Lena did what she did.

My personal experiences with compasses have not ended as well as Lardy's, who eventually convinced his beloved a two-year absence was not all that unusual for a compass-impaired man lost on a large body of water. Like my friend, I always carried a compass, but there were problems because compasses didn't make a lick of sense. Over the years, I had observed the needle always pointed north, but a lot of undesirable destinations—like Siberia were to the north, and by following the red arrow, I had almost been there twice. Employers had a difficult time comprehending this enervation, and on both occasions I returned to find I was no longer expected to attend the company picnic.

As with my waders and my gloves, I can still access my compass should I desire, and I admit I still entertain the hope that one day when I'm desperately lost on some high-mountain grouse road, I will dig it from under the seat and make it work. It isn't realistic, but most fantasies aren't, and I know that even from the coffin, Grandpa would gnash his gums if he thought I was being wasteful.

Inland Tuna

Thirty-six years ago, my father sold me into summer slavery to an orchardist in Penewawa, Washington. I was 17 and unemployed—a combination I liked a lot but my father deeply resented. Raised during the Depression, Dad "worked 28 hours a day, lived on tripe and rabbit kidneys, and didn't sleep, smile, or look at girls" the entire time. There was no way a son of his would sit idly about and enjoy the summer when there were dollars and calluses to be made.

Being slave to an orchardist wasn't easy, even if the orchard was situated on the banks of the Snake River near some of the best smallmouth bass fishing in the state. My work day began at six a.m. when I moved two lines of sprinklers in the lower pasture, and it ended at seven p.m. when I moved them again. Between those times, I thinned apricots or peaches, fixed fence, put up hay, cut weeds, and felt sorry for myself because the pay was bad and the work/play ratio was way out of whack.

When the fruit ripened, I was expected to haul it to the packing shed, help sort it into boxes I had built, and then load it on the truck for delivery into town. The only thing I didn't do was pick; that job was reserved for transient laborers like Shorty Nevdahl.

Shorty had been coming to the Penewawa orchards every July and August for seven years. Initially, he had been sort of shanghaied from a Spokane tavern, loaded aboard a cattle truck, and dumped at the ranch. When he sobered up 40 miles from the nearest bottle of Tokay, he was disoriented and hungry, and as there didn't seem to be a bus between Penewawa and town, he reluctantly decided to pick apricots for $7.50 a day until he could make good his escape.

After three days, Shorty decided he liked picking apricots, or rather he liked the regular meals and the proximity to the Snake River. He finished out the apricot harvest, came back with a fishing pole for the peach harvest, and then showed up regularly every year after that.

Until I met Shorty, I knew nothing whatsoever about women, and politics, and darn little about angling. Learning—lots of it—took place under his tutelage, though much of what I learned was probably a matter of fantasy and strong opinion rather than fact. Practically the only useful knowledge Shorty transferred to my adolescent brain was that squawfish are not bad fish.

Every state has a squawfish. It may be called by a different name with more political correctness, or even be a different fish, but its primary characteristics are homeliness, boniness, and a bad reputation. Sucker. Gar. Chub. Minnow. As a kid, I threw them on the bank. Some states have even paid bounties. No one practiced catch and release on "trash fish" such as these.

But Shorty was different. Shorty said he was getting too old to "go 'round playin' God." If he couldn't keep a fish for the frying pan, it went back into the water. "Eatin' a fish," he told me, "makes sense. That's why they're here. I aint a-throwin' it back if I can eat it, but I aint about to kill it if I can't."

Mostly, Shorty ate the squawfish he caught. Furthermore, he taught a lot of others to eat it, too. On Sundays when the owners allowed no work around the ranch, the laborers were given only a late breakfast and a "supper" which came in mid-afternoon. On those days, a man could get mighty hungry along about eight p.m., so on those days Shorty headed to the river, fished a couple hours, and returned to the bunkhouse with a huge stringer of northern squawfish. These he filleted, scored with a sharp knife to break up the bones, rolled in corn meal and salt, and fried in butter in a cast iron griddle over a hot plate. I have never tasted better fish.

In the years since Shorty, I have learned a lot about fishing, and I have also unlearned a lot of things he taught me. Smallmouth, I discovered, do not turn to largemouth when they mature. Carp are not orange like goldfish when they are young, and a catfish cannot sting you with his whiskers. I have also discovered that age, besides making your eyes go goofy, does indeed make one look more closely at the inviolability of life.

I'll still keep a mess of fish when I get the hankering, and when it comes to pickling, I'd rather have squawfish than anything. Sometimes I go fishing just *for* squawfish or suckers because they're big, there's no limit, and they're fun to catch. If you're partial to smoked, canned salmon, smoked, canned sucker is nearly as tasty, and the fish cakes rival the best from any "game fish."

A friend of mine, Jim Deniston, has even solved the "reputation" problem resulting from years of piscatorial discrimination. "Just change the name," he told me. "My wife wouldn't eat a squawfish on a bet. She's just wild about 'inland tuna', though."

From the Desk of Alan Liere

Dear Dr. McNumnenson:

Three days ago I received my Patient Report from Inland Imaging, and I have been trying to get in touch with you ever since. As you will recall, I have had a tingling in my upper back and neck ever since the last day of the '97-'98 waterfowl season when I grounded my boat on that mud flat in the Pend Oreille River. Lacey insisted I have it looked at, but I'm sure I mentioned to you that it was probably just a strain.

Evidently, Dr McNumnenson, you forgot to pass that information on to Bernard, your X-Ray technician, because according to the report I now have in front of me, "There is clear evidence of subscapular atrophy as well as large anterior osteophytes and sclerosis at the C1-2 joint." Well, Lacey saw the report before I did, and her imagination ran wild when she read Bernard's interpretation. It took a medical dictionary and a fair piece of fancy talking before she would sleep in the same room with me again.

Unless I've missed my bet, all that medical jargon translates to "My sister, the physical therapist, just bought a condominium and she wants you to pay for it," the "you" in this case being me. I don't think that will be happening, Dr. McNumnenson, and you can tell Bernard so, too. I would like to know how in heaven's name anyone thought I could be afflicted by even one of those ten-dollar words just because I grounded my boat on a mud flat.

Dr. McNumnenson, this report also says I have uncovertebral spondylosis. That is incorrect. I had an Uncle Dixie once who used to drive a convertible, but he put it through the ice on Moses Lake during the winter of '58, and we never saw it again. Sadly, we never saw Uncle Dixie again, either. You would have liked him, Dr. McNumnenson. He was a waterfowl hunter, like you and me, and quite a cut-up. He used to put the top down and drive that old car right out into the middle of one of his big stands of unharvested field corn. When the ducks weren't flying, he'd eat a bag of Chee-tos and listen to Elvis on the radio. I don't know if such a car blind would be legal today—maybe it wasn't legal back then. At the very least, there's probably some kind of permit that would need to be purchased, and a couple dozen forms to fill out. It's pretty amazing how many questionable acts become okay if you just do the paperwork.

I appreciate your concern regarding my increased poundage, but I can explain, and I'm surprised you had to ask. The last time you put me on the scales was right at the end of the hunting season. Well, my waterfowling weight is about 209, but in the off-season when I'm not tossing decoys, building blinds, laying on my back in wet pea fields, and getting my boat unstuck, I shoot up to about 235. I try to hold that weight, then, through the summer, because once the October duck opener rolls around, I'm sure to become anorexic again.

About my blood pressure: this Patient Report here says it is currently 130 over 80, though I must admit I have never understood those numbers. The report also suggests that 130 over 80 is pretty good for a man my age. A MAN MY AGE! What do they mean by that, Dr. McNumnenson? Eons ago, a lady told me I was a pretty fair dancer for the shape I was in, and I still haven't figured out if she was talking about my general well-being or the shape I was in that particular night. Then, a few years back, when I tried my hand at trap shooting, the boys at the range told me I was a decent shot—considering. Considering? Considering my age? Considering the shape I'm in? Considering the fact I shoot a 30-year-old full choke side by side with camo tape on the barrels?

And speaking of a full choke, Dr. McNumnenson, I think Bernard would benefit from one. The last time I was in, I considered giving him a half nelson and an Indian rub, but now I'm convinced a two-handed grip around his Adam's apple is the only answer. The main problem is that little gown he always has me put on backwards like a cape. Why, pray tell, did I have to put the thing on for a neck X-Ray? Makes no more sense than the time your nurse had me take off my clothes so she could draw blood. And why did Bernard insist I call him Robin? Talk to him, will you, Dr. McNumnenson?

There's one last thing I'd like to question you on, and that's my bill. The one your secretary gave me says I owe $85 for an office call. During that "office call," I sat in the waiting room for 45 minutes and on the edge of an examination room table for another 15. Then, you came in, asked a few questions, poked around a little, and said "Uh-huh" a couple times. You next inquired about my hunting season and I explained to you how to put out a deep-water set for bluebills. That took 15 minutes, and then you sent me down for X-Rays. By my calculations, you owe me for an hour and a quarter and I owe you for three minutes. I'm willing to call it even. Always happy to extend a professional courtesy to another waterfowl hunter.

Best wishes,

Alan Liere

The Bomb

Gray-rusted and ominous, the bomb lay on the fringes of an overgrown railroad right-away on the south end of town. Nearly obscured by tangled vetch and wild rose, it would have probably gone undiscovered yet another year had the stone, thrown in boredom at a scolding magpie, not gone astray, clanking against the metal.

It was late spring, he was nine, and the weekend offered a short reprieve from school. But even a Saturday and a Sunday could do little to help him forget the confining, sand-colored walls of Miss Orvik's fourth-grade class. Within that stockade, the "smart kids" were allowed to clean erasers and set up painting easels and the "slow" ones such as he, who lacked the motivation rather than the intelligence to make a hundred divide by four without a remainder, toiled facelessly under the yoke of Group Four. Painfully shy, he was also painfully aware he was missing that nebulous, enigmatic parent the other kids called "Dad" or "Pops" or "my old man."

Until he found the bomb, his life had been little more than a routine, and the sameness tainted even the weekends. Six days a week, his mother worked part time in a little tourist shop down town, and because he had gotten used to it, he arose early with her. Even when there was no school, he was out of the house by eight. This spring day he wandered as usual without purpose toward the park, then away from town on the tracks—first scuffing along in the gravel, eventually balancing on the rails, pretending he was on a narrow bridge high above a raging river. That first metallic clank from the weeds, however, changed everything, and he spent the remainder of the afternoon studying the rusted gray form from a safe distance, trying to muster the courage to go closer.

He knew it was a bomb, and he knew bombs killed people. Once, long ago, he had wondered if that, perhaps, was what had killed his "Dad" or "Pops" or "old man." He had, after all, heard his mother say something about bombs when she spoke about a terrible place called Vietnam that had changed her life forever. His Aunt Linda, though, didn't mention bombs; she made vague, whispered references to alcoholism and a court martial and "better off without him." And that was all he knew. Still, he decided, it had been a bomb—a big, gray one just like the one in the patch of purple vetch.

That night at dinner, he told his mother.

"A bomb, huh?" she said, her eyes on the Six O'Clock News.

"A real bomb," he said, trying to make himself sit bigger on the stool. "Out by the tracks."

"A real bomb, huh?" she repeated, flicking up the volume with the remote control and looking beyond him at a fashionably-dressed female reporter who was sticking a microphone into the face of a very angry-looking politician.

"Yeah," he said softly. "Out by the tracks." Then, he excused himself and went through the back door into the street where he kicked a deflated basketball around for a couple hours before returning to his room and early bed.

The next morning, he was out of the house before his mother, and when the church bells announced the start of Sunday school, he was leaning against a stump on the other end of town, studying the bomb in the railroad right-of-way. For a long time, he watched it thus, and when the sun climbed higher above the horizon, its warmth awakened the mosquitoes, and he held his breath when a yellow and gray bird appeared from nowhere and perched defiantly atop the lethal hunk of metal, searching the tall weeds for its breakfast. Creeping cautiously closer, the boy shooed the bird, then waited another five minutes to see if his intervention had changed anything. When the time had passed, he began to toss small pebbles, trying on one hand to hit the bomb but fearful on the other of what would happen if he succeeded. With each metallic "tink," he cringed and promised he would not do it again, but he always did, and as the morning slid into afternoon, the pebbles were thrown with more confidence and velocity. Still, he could not muster the courage to go closer.

"The bomb rattles," he told his mother that night over dinner. "If I hit it with a rock, it rattles."

"You probably broke it," she said instinctively, her mouth full of frozen pot pie. She wasn't really listening, though, and the TV nearly drowned her voice.

"Tomorrow I'll touch it," he said.

"Be careful," she replied absently.

At exactly ten o'clock the next morning, the attendance secretary called the mother at the little tourist shop in town. Her son was not at school. Was he ill?

"He left before I did," the mother said. She also started to say he never missed school and should be there, but realized how silly that would sound. Then, a horrible, vague recollection made her squeeze the receiver. What was that he had been jabbering about the night before at dinner?

They found him motionless in the weeds of the railroad right-of-way, slumped forward in an awkward, rag-doll sitting position. The school principal and the sheriff tried to hold her back, but the mother ran hysterically toward her son, wailing his name.

Just before she would have fallen beside him, he became aware of her presence. Snapping his head upward, his wide, brown eyes met hers, and he was afraid. Rising timidly, he brushed the dirt and weed stems from his pants and looked around. "Why's everybody here?" he asked. Then, he saw his principal. "I guess I'm a little late, huh?"

His mother drew him to her. "A lot late, mister," she said. Then, she began to sob.

"But lookee here, Mom," he said, noting her distress but overcome with his own excitement. He indicated the rusted, gray, metal box next to him. "It's full of fishin' stuff, Mom. Wasn't no bomb a'tall."

She pulled one of his hands into hers, rubbing it softly. Tears streaked her face, making little rivulets that carried mascara almost comically past the corners of her mouth. "Looks just like your dad's," she sniffed. "Exactly like your dad's."

The boy flinched. This—all of it—was new to him. Gently, he pulled away, kneeled before the open tackle box, and touched a tarnished lure with a green-plastic insert. "I didn't know he fished," he said softly. "I didn't know nothin' for sure."

"He loved to fish," she whispered, kneeling beside him. "He was good at it, too. Before he was drafted, we'd drive out to the end of the road and fish the farm pond for bullheads or punkinseed sunfish—just the two of us. Sometimes we'd stay out most all night, just listening to the frogs and the crickets and wondering what the poor people were doing."

"Couldn't we do that, too?" the boy asked shyly, very much aware of the presence of the others. "Just you and me? I mean, some of this stuff is kinda rusted and all, but some of it will clean up pretty new, I think. Maybe you and me could go out after work some time and wonder 'bout the poor people."

The sheriff and the principal and most of the gawkers were headed back to their cars. His mother gently closed the gray box. "I think I'd like that." She smiled and tousled his hair, then helped him to his feet. "And your dad would like it too." She tapped the box affectionately with her toe. "He would for a fact. I just know he would."

Lumbago, She Says

I had always been a little less than forgiving to drivers who appeared to talk to themselves, a curiosity I witnessed most often at stop lights here in town. Oh sure, it had been brought to my attention that some of these eccentrics were merely singing along with the car radio, but I was nevertheless amused when I encountered what I called "vehicular monologues." My usual reaction was to lean forward and stare at the offender until my presence was realized, then smirk, shake my head, and drive slowly away as the light changed, feeling ever-so-smug. This small meanness often made my day, and I convinced myself that everyone was better off because I was on a monologue alert.

On the way home from a fishing trip a few years ago, I was horrified to discover *I* was talking to myself. Or at least, I was in the incipient stages of talking to myself. I had been driving silently along in the rain, staring dumbly into the glaring eight o' clock headlights, when someone in my vehicle distinctly uttered the phrase, "Lumbago, she says." A quick check confirmed the fact the "someone" was I, and a brief analysis resulted in the puzzled admission I had no idea what the phrase meant. I didn't, in fact, even know what lumbago was. Oops, I thought. Must be getting tired. Well, that won't happen again and no harm done, as no one saw my lips move.

To my relief, that was the last time I ever mentioned lumbago. To my chagrin, however, there was another outburst a few weeks later in the middle of a solo, early-morning drive to a bass lake when I exclaimed out of the blue, "This old house!" After admonishing myself (also out loud), I drove on a few miles and calmly said it again! Its origins were a total mystery. This incident was followed by several others over a period of five months, and by the beginning of autumn, I was speaking to myself in complete sentences, none of which had any substance, and all of which caught me by surprise. The one I remember best slid from my lips just as I pulled into the launch at Waitts Lake: "But what about the dahlias, Mr. Reebok?" Utterances such as this certainly eliminated the possibility I was *thinking* out loud.

Until just recently, there had been no witnesses to my vehicular monologues. Coming either after dark, before dawn, or on back roads, they usually had something to do with a fishing trip, and I do a lot of my fishing alone. Last week, however, my wife, Lacey, accompanied me on an exploratory smallmouth expedition, and in the middle of extended silences, I erupted twice, once with "Are there olives on your sandwich, sir?" and once with "Tell the coach I'll be there by eight." The first time, Lacey merely looked at me sleepily and answered "No," but the second time she wanted to know just which coach I was talking about and if I was referring to eight a.m. or eight p.m.

"Sorry," I said sheepishly. "Just thinking out loud."

"About what, dear?" she asked.

"Well. . . .about coaches, of course," I said defensively. Lacey was eyeing me the way she does when she finds I have put my dirty underwear in the refrigerator rather than the clothes hamper.

"Do your coaches like olives?" she asked sweetly.

It was no use. Lacey can detect a deception quicker than a dog finds a rotting carp. "Dear," I said timidly, "do you ever just talk to yourself?"

My wife looked at me sympathetically and nuzzled closer. "Is that what this is all about?" she purred. "Have you started talking to yourself?"

I fidgeted uncomfortably. "It's kind of embarrassing," I said. "I mean—all these years I've made fun of people who talk to themselves, and now I'm starting to do it, too."

"Alan," Lacey said, "there is nothing wrong with talking to yourself. Saying something out loud is a good way to remember it. It is an excellent way of verifying your existence. Talking to yourself increases your confidence. A thought is just a thought, but once you say it out loud, it can become a fact."

"I never considered that," I said. "And thanks; it makes me feel better." I smiled at my spouse. "Many of the things I say don't make any sense, though," I confessed.

Lacey smiled back and said nothing.

"Really," I continued. "And that bothers me. Sometimes I say stuff that has no relevance to anything."

"Everything has relevance," Lacey said. "Sometimes the loop from here to there is lengthy, but one thing always leads to another. Sometimes you will be led into an area that doesn't seem remotely related to your verbalization, but once you're there, you'll see the connection." She leaned forward in the truck and tried to read a road sign. "You missed the turn-off," she said "I thought we were going fishing."

"Thanks again, dear," I said. "I feel a lot better. For a while there, I thought I was going goofy. You can't imagine what a relief it is to know *you*, at least, accept my little eccentricity."

Lacey patted my hand and smiled benevolently, and I didn't worry about my "problem" until later that week when I was at a stop light in town rehearsing what I would say to the store clerk who had just sold me four-pound monofilament when I requested eight. In the midst of a rather animated monologue, I became aware that the driver of the car next to me was staring. I leaned back, sheepishly trying to become part of the upholstery. Then I realized the other driver was my wife. I started to wave, but the light changed. She smirked, shook her head, and drove slowly off.

Evolution Of A Hunter

Unless I count my Great Uncle Harliss, who was detained for a week in the Grant County jail for dispatching a neighbor's noisy rooster with a two-hand scythe, there were, I've been told, no sportsmen among my ancestors. And considering the fact I never hefted a real gun until I was nearly 16, it is puzzling, indeed, that I evolved into a hunter.

The truth is, I don't know why I subject myself each autumn to the pain and humiliation of hunting. The need to do so is simply something I awoke with one morning after ninth-grade graduation—kind of like what happened one day four years earlier when I fell asleep in the back yard reading *Tarzan of the Apes* and woke up wondering if the 12-year-old girl next door was a good kisser. As near as I can figure, though, the origins of my hunting spirit can be traced to weed bombs, road apples, and Giant Jenny.

From earliest childhood, the noises made by projectiles were a source of auditory captivation. Dirt clods and "weed bombs" were my first missiles because my family lived next door to a vacant lot that held a prodigious supply of both. Weed bombs were clumps of dry cheat grass pulled up carefully by the roots in late summer so the crumbly soil remained attached. Flung with an overhand arc like a grenade, the "bombs" made an absolutely delightful *whoompff* when smashed against the neighbor's garage. If I threw them in a modified arc, I could achieve decent accuracy and enough velocity to produce an impressive cloud of "smoke."

Now, the side of the neighbor's garage didn't demand much in the way of accuracy, but once in a wonderful while, Davey Williams' dog—the one that had eaten my hamster, Art—would slink down the alley, and I delighted in paying him back for his transgression. Sometimes, when the memory of Art's demise was particularly wrenching and Davey's dog particularly close, I would substitute dirt clods for weed bombs because they didn't require an overhand lob. A good-sized dirt clod could settle any number of old scores, and I was always impressed with the solid whhooommpfff! the clod made on impact. The "*yi-yi-yi* " of the dog wasn't bad, either.

When I graduated from dirt, I became involved briefly with rocks. But rocks were too unforgiving for a six-year-old, and I didn't like the sound they made when they ricocheted off a telephone pole and through a garage window. The owners of the garage windows didn't think much of it, either.

After rocks, I moved on to chuckin' sticks. A chuckin' stick created a variety of tantalizing whooshes and thunks, depending on the length of the stick and the nature of the ammunition. Basically, a chuckin' stick was a smooth tree branch 1/2 to one inch in diameter and anywhere from two to four feet long. The thin end was whittled sharp, ammunition was impaled on the point, and the stick was then whipped with both hands from a spot beginning somewhere behind the shoulder. *Whooosssh.*

Green apples were the best projectiles for chuckin' sticks, as they made a healthy *smaaack!* on impact. With a four-foot chucker I'd dubbed Miss Flossie because it was shaped like my second-grade teacher, I created a lot of nervous tension among the magpies that were forever raiding my cat's food dish on the back porch. Had I not run out of green apples, it is quite possible I would have become an Olympic-caliber chucker. After a cool spring, however, Mrs. Collett's apple tree failed to bloom, and that summer I was forced to use what was euphemistically known as "road apples." Road apples were not as abundant in suburbia as, say, yellow delicious, but if you looked hard enough, you could always find a few along Queen Street after old man Simms had driven his horses home from a landscaping job.

There were problems, too, with road apples; they often broke apart prematurely, they always made a displeasing, soft *spa-whaack* on impact, and they had to be aged before seeing action. Mom was more than a little put out when she discovered I was doing the aging in a shoe box in my closet. It was she who suggested I make a slingshot.

It didn't take me long to become enraptured by this primitive weapon, either. I loved the *twaanng* I could get from a slingshot, and like the rest of my arsenal, they were cheap—they grew on trees. Although I had seen advertisements for commercially manufactured models, I doubted anyone would actually spend good money for something there for the cutting. A medium-sized willow, after all, could arm every kid in town.

Actually, my very first slingshot wasn't even made of wood. I discovered that by stretching a rubber band between my index finger and my thumb, I could propel a small piece of folded paper with considerable accuracy. It was this "finger rocket," in fact, that accompanied me on my first real hunting expeditions as I stalked flies in the back of my fourth-grade classroom. A folded gum wrapper was deadly at three inches, but greater distances required using the gum itself to attain the necessary trajectory and velocity. I preferred the gum loads because they provided an aesthetic *spa-laaack* (not to be confused with *spa-whaack*) as well as adherent properties. My most memorable shot was the one I made with a wad of Bazooka bubble gum on a buzzing blue bottle fly; I not only nailed the critter in mid-air, I stuck him to the window. It was my first wing shot and an easy retrieve.

Giant Jenny was the great-grandmother of my finger rockets, the climax of two years of creative slingshottery. For 30 years, she had been a crab apple tree on my uncle's farm overlooking the Big Spokane River. Then, my cousin, Raymond, and I decided one spring morning she needed some pruning, and with saws and hatchets we reduced her to a trunk and two limbs. We tried to explain to my Uncle Oscar that we'd only meant to be helpful; the fact his crab apple tree looked like a giant Y was an indication of our gardening inexperience rather than evidence of some ulterior motive. Uncle Oscar didn't buy it, but the damage was done. When Raymond and I were no longer grounded, the world's biggest slingshot was still there in the back yard. The temptation was overwhelming, and we proceeded with our original plan.

Raymond, his younger brother, Albert, and I, tied four old inner tubes together, spliced a large square of steer hide in the middle as a pouch, and wired each end to opposite sides of the fork. With the three of us pulling, we could stretch the tubes back seven feet and launch a baseball-sized rock a hundred yards into the river where a flock of mergansers often sat. *Tuuunnnng*. The stone would hum out and upward and land with a *tunk*, followed by a geyser of water.

Had we stuck to rocks, I imagine Giant Jenny would still be around. Uncle Oscar, however, chopped her down right after Raymond and I tried to launch Albert into the river. Thinking back on the incident, I often wonder if his reaction would have been as severe had Albert cleared the fork and splashed down with the mergansers. I think he might have been impressed by that. As it was, the sight of his youngest son crumpled and gasping at the base of a butchered crab apple tree didn't make Uncle Oscar very happy.

Afterward, Raymond told me his dad wouldn't have been nearly so upset had I not insisted on tying Albert up before the attempted lift-off. I guess Raymond had forgotten Albert hadn't exactly volunteered for the mission, and it had taken both of us the better part of an hour to run him into a corner.

A paper route and the demise of Giant Jenny eventually tempered my experiments with homemade launching devices. Finding myself suddenly wealthy at age ten, I purchased an eight-dollar bow and three arrows and gave all my slingshots, plastic-straw blowguns, and a box of road apples to Davey Williams. I figured he and his dog had a vested interest in them anyway. I did keep the "crossbow" I had fashioned from a ping pong paddle and the elastic from my dad's underwear, and it's still here in a box of good stuff from my youth. Sometimes, when I'm cleaning my .270 or planning another caribou hunt in Alaska, I take it out and wonder if the Bengal tigers are still there in the alley behind my old house.

Bird Brains

Given the greater capacity of the human cranium, one would rightfully assume man capable of out-thinking a bird. Match Homo Sapiens against a pheasant or a chukar in a game of Trivial Pursuit or Chess, for example, and nine out of ten times the winner will not have feathers.

Further testimony to man's assumed superiority over fowl in the thinking department is evidenced by the term "bird brain," a designation coined to describe someone who orders corn dogs at a fancy restaurant when the other guy is paying.

The problem with thinking is that it is usually over-cooked. Oddly enough, over-cooking a thought frequently results in half-baked conclusions and silly actions. In my years of hunting, I've seen birds fooled, but I have never seen one make a fool of itself. For the hunter afield, however, that is an everyday occurrence.

Once, on a chukar hill in eastern Washington, struggling in stocking feet toward my truck with the remains of a new pair of cowboy boots under my arm, I perceived two red spheres floating toward me. I briefly contemplated the terrifying possibility I would be swept up by extraterrestrial beings, whisked away to an alien planet, and made to take third grade over again from Miss Fitz. Miss Fitz had hated me for what she termed my "debauched and licentious" insistence on rhyming her name with a certain, outhouse noun in an off-color playground ballad I had made up and liked to sing. She always swore she'd get even, and the fact she didn't has caused me to look nervously over my shoulder ever since. Perhaps that was her plan.

Anyway, seconds after seeing the spheres, I met two chukar hunters with red helium balloons attached by long strings to their belts. Politely ignoring my wisecracks about birthday parties, they explained they were using the chukars' natural fear of raptors to their advantage. They theorized that if a soaring hawk could cause a covey of partridge to freeze, so could a hovering helium balloon. No chukar, after all, had ever attended the county fair or the circus, and bobbing balloons would represent danger from above. Their natural instinct would be to hunker down.

"Doing any good?" I asked.

"Put up a couple coveys," one answered.

"Close?" I asked.

"Not exactly," the other admitted. "I don't think the balloons are having much effect."

"Yeah," I said seriously, "I think I'd go with yellow next time."

Both of them were looking upward with puzzled expressions as we parted, and I didn't feel nearly so foolish to be again picking my way through a low cactus patch in dirty gray and green tube socks.

Another example of man's tendency to over-think to the point of silliness was witnessed this last November during the pheasant season. Having labored up a cheat grass hillside to the stubble above, I was surprised to see four shotgunners ambling toward me in a line, spread out to cover an acre of cover, and connected by an umbilical cord of white twine. Marbles rolled around in tin cans hanging from this lifeline at 20-foot intervals, creating a sound very much like that of marbles rolling around in tin cans. I was immediately struck with the resemblance to a "telephone" my boyhood chum, Eddie, and I had once devised using a long piece of string and empty Dixie Cups.

"Expecting a call?" I asked as they came closer.

The man on my end raised his hand, and all four came to a halt. "This wasn't my idea," he said sheepishly, jerking his thumb to the right. "Rudy, down there, figured this one out. He said we could cover more ground and flush more pheasants."

"Any luck?" I asked.

"Are you kidding?" he spat. "So far we've spent an hour hunting and two hours trying to get this mess through the fences. I haven't seen so many tangles since I took my three-year-old fishing, and the birds are **still** running out the other end."

"You ought to try putting a transistor radio at the end of the field," I told him. "A little music will stop them every time."

His face brightened. "Hey, that's not bad!" he grinned. "I'll tell Rudy."

Seeing my insights were no longer needed, I wished him luck and started back down the hill.

"Hey, mister," he called when I was 60 yards away, "What station?"

"Doesn't matter as long as it's country," I hollered back. "Those China birds just love a good clothespin singer."

"Clothespin singer?"

"Yeah—you know—someone that sounds like he's got a clothespin on his nose. Someone with a good twang."

I turned again and contemplated my next move. With all the competition, I figured it might be a good time to try the new pheasant call I had invented. How could a bird resist a yelper that sounded like a kernel of wheat?

Lacey's Featherbed

Behind his store in Cato, Missouri, population six, my Uncle Olander and Aunt Ruthie lived in a big, white house. I remember it as two-story and auspicious with cupolas and pillars and all sorts of *Gone with the Wind* architecture, though my parents' old scrapbook shows pictures of a rather modest, unpainted abode with chickens in the yard and a two-holer off to one side. Aunt Ruthie relaxes on the sagging front steps, flashing those too-perfect dentures—exactly the way I remember her the autumn of '54 when our family drove south to visit my mother's side of the woodpile.

Behind Aunt Ruthie in a corner of the enclosed porch is the featherbed. She had sewn the twilled ticking herself and stuffed it with the down and breast feathers of her own chickens. "'Bout a thousand Leghorns in there," she'd grunt each time we drug the heavy thing out, "and dern near as many hours." Then she'd fluff it up and tuck me in. Bed time at Aunt Ruthie's was the only time in my young life I didn't mind the lights going off. Following a day of farm chores and fishin' poles, I could kiss her good-night and succumb wearily to the protective folds of soft feathers. Peering upward, I could then puzzle out the constellations through the screen and listen as a symphony of small night creatures performed for a smiling moon. If anything, sleep came too quickly.

Forty years after that glorious autumn sojourn, I bought my

wife, Lacey, a featherbed for her birthday. Perhaps it was selfish of me to attempt to thus recapture an important part of my childhood, but Lacey was excited by my gift, even though it was an anemic, store-bought, four-inch-thick imposter of the massive creation I really desired.

"I knew you'd like it," I smiled when she opened the package. "I remembered what you said about your grandmother's farm and that big blue-ticked featherbed you used to sleep on."

Lacey frowned. "My grandmother's farm? My grandmother lived in a condominium in Seattle."

"But I remember something about feathers," I said.

"It was a boa," Lacey said. "A feather boa. Grams always wore it when she went to play Bingo."

"Oh."

"But thanks just the same, dear," she said. "This looks delicious." She carried the package upstairs and I could hear her whistling as she remade the bed.

Lacey was already tucked snugly away when I got there, and the mattress did, indeed, look delicious. I climbed in, then lay back to await the magic, but something was poking me between my shoulder blades. I rolled to my stomach. Now something was sticking me just below the navel. "Lacey," I said at last, "are you comfortable?"

My wife stirred slightly and sighed.

"Lacey," I said, "There's a feather poking me through the cover."

"Hmmmmmmm."

I tried again to get comfortable. A gap between the featherbed and the wall had swallowed my pillow. I fought the sticky, confining bulk, trying once more to roll over. Every time I moved, the bed crackled and poked me. "Lacey," I said angrily, "there's a whole darn chicken in here."

"Hmmmmm."

"I'm not kidding, Lacey. I can feel a leg and a wing bone. Might be a gizzard here, too." I was suffocating in feathers. I got up, opened a window, and stared at the distant lights of the city. Then I lay down again. A night breeze slammed the bedroom door with a BANG! Lacey didn't stir. As I contemplated this injustice, the room cooled off. I closed the window and tried again to entice the sandman. Too hot. I opened the window. Too cold. Close the window. Open the window. Under the covers. Atop the covers. Repeat. I was waiting for something—a feeling, I think, but it wasn't there. Where were the frogs and katydids and the stars that settled like Christmas lights in the branches of Aunt Ruthie's red oak? Had I hoped to elude my own, adult bogeymen (who now came in both business suits and mechanic's coveralls)? I propped my pillow against the wall and sat up. In deep repose next to me, Lacey practically purred with contentment. It was a very long night.

"Did you ever get to sleep?" my wife asked me the next morning over coffee and the Tribune. "I heard that window shut a dozen times."

"Didn't think you'd noticed," I grumbled, staring into the depths of the cup and preparing to be pathetic.

Lacey held her mug with both hands and smiled at me above the steaming rim. "I'm sorry," she said sympathetically. "I slept wonderfully. I can't remember ever feeling so. . . ."

". . .so safe?" I interrupted hopefully.

". . .so sleepy," Lacey continued. "I tried to stay awake to. . . "

" . . .watch the stars?" I blurted.

". . .talk to you about the septic tank," she said. "You know it's making that awful stench again." She looked at me warily.

I guessed I wouldn't ask her about the katydids.

A Matter Of Adaptability

Following six weeks and several hundred dollars worth of professional obedience training, my Uncle Al's "bird dog," Sherman, had still not gotten over a tendency to act dumb when Uncle Al gave a command. Personally, I think, this was due to Sherman's lineage, which is part spaniel, part mongrel, and part Nubian goat, but I imagine it also has something to do with the fact that the man who "trained" him was the same fellow arrested last year for a roofing scam.

One thing about Uncle Al, though—he does not lack persistence. Uncle Al has been working with Sherman himself, and just recently was able to brag that his dog has evolved into a model of compliance.

"It's just a matter of adapting to the situation," Al said, dragging Sherman to the middle of the kitchen floor. "Now watch this."

Removing the leash, he stepped back from the slobbering canine, and Sherman instantly flopped to the linoleum and began unrolling his prodigious tongue. "**Lay down, Sherman**," Uncle Al commanded loudly, beaming with pride as the already-lounging dog remained in that position.

Then, without command, Sherman stood up. "**Don't lay down, Sherman**," Uncle Al said. The pathetic creature stood staring at us dumbly with his little goat eyes, then sat down and began to scratch. "**Sit**," AL said quickly. Then, he turned to me.

"See?" he said. "It's just a matter of being adaptable."
"And fast," I replied.

Actually, I learned a long time ago that being adaptable is almost as good as being proficient. I, for example, am what my wife and assorted hunting and fishing buddies refer to (depending on what they have had for breakfast) as "mechanically disinclined," "Mr. Badwrench," or "You dumb expletive!" I once "cured" a double-barrel of firing both barrels at once with some intricate jiggling. Afterwards, the first barrel went off when I closed the breech, and the second wouldn't fire at all.

For my wife, I "fixed" an electric frying pan, and when she plugged it in, the shower of sparks fused the handle to the toaster. My attempts to install a sprinkling system made the water in the bath tub come on every morning at three a.m. The fact is, I have never been able to tell the difference between positive and negative, screws and bolts, Tab A and Slot B, or even right and left. But adaptable? Boy, am I adaptable! The electric frying pan, minus the handle, is now a storage container for my fly line, the double gun on the wall of my den serves as a pretty fair indicator of when the room needs dusting, and all that expensive water pipe and fittings I bought make a great frame for the camouflage on my duck boat.

Being adaptable has become increasingly handy during my lengthy stint as an outdoorsman-impersonator, particularly during my impersonations of a fisherman. Most men would be upset to arrive at their favorite steelheading river and find they have been dragging a favorite rod by a tangle of mono behind the truck. Not me. A seven-foot steelhead rod, if drug far enough, makes a wonderful carp spear.

My ability to adapt began at an early age. On my eighth birthday, my father gave me my very own fishing reel. Two days later, I had taken it apart to see what made the clicking sound inside when a certain button was pushed. Generally, a child's interest in such things indicates a degree of mechanical aptitude, and his parents will gloat and make ambitious predictions about his future as an aerospace engineer. Mine knew better, though, as the garage floor was already littered with radio parts that would never again be part of a whole, and several wheeled devices that worked only in reverse. That reel, like many I have since owned, had a handful of leftover parts. Reassembled, it made a pretty decent paperweight, and for the next five years, my only "fishing reel" was a tin can wrapped with nylon line.

Outboard motors have always tested my ability to adapt to stressful situations. Usually, they have made me a still fisherman when I had intended to be a troller, or a castaway where I had intended to make one quick loop around the island and return to camp before lunch. They have also provided me the opportunity to test my proficiency with grappling hooks. Sometimes, I even make a game of this activity, involving as many others as possible by offering a cash reward to the one who can retrieve the submerged six-horse before it is covered with barnacles. Afterwards, if the grappling is unsuccessful and the motor belongs to my neighbor, Durwood Pickle, I can check my performance in the 40-yard sprint as I attempt to outrun the heavy glass ashtray Durwood now puts in his back pocket when he sees me coming up the steps.

Last year on Loon Lake, I was particularly pleased to be using my new, light-weight, four-horse outboard. Mike, Ed, and I were on a mackinaw-fishing expedition in heavy swells when the thing quit running. Had it been any heavier, my boat would have surely gone bow over stern when they attacked me with bailing buckets for putting their lives in jeopardy.

That weekend, from beginning to end, tested my adaptability to the limit. It is extremely difficult to feign conviviality when your fishing partners are threatening to tie you up and set you adrift on a leaky air mattress.

The motor, incidentally, adapted quite well to its new role as an anchor.

A Sigh For March

Though I have sometimes pooh-poohed the same tendency in others, I have always had a superstitious bent. Just a little one. Certainly, I do not believe in black cats and bad luck, or step-on-a-crack, break your mother's back, but I am a little reluctant to gas up at pump 13 on Friday the 13th, and I always hang my horseshoes pointing up.

Most of all, I play counting games with headlights (please don't ask), and I am careful to never heave a premature sigh of relief. In my book, heaving a sigh of relief is as good as a guarantee that the monster you thought you had foiled is still waiting behind the bath robe in the closet. Heaving a sigh of relief after safely navigating a treacherous, ice-covered section of highway is like tantalizing some unknown force to suck you into the closed garage door as you pull onto the pad. It's like saying to your wife, "Boy, I'm glad *that's* over," only to find it isn't.

By March, I'm tempted to say, "Whew, I'm sure glad THAT winter is behind us!" I'm afraid to, though, because a few years back, in February, I mentioned with a big sigh to a neighbor that we had made it through the winter. The next morning my truck was high-centered in my driveway in 30 inches of drifted snow, and it stayed that way for nearly two weeks.

Since Lacey and I moved to the country, getting cars back up our driveway in the winter has become one of my most enduring tasks. This wouldn't be so bad if only our personal vehicles were involved, but I am also responsible for the vehicles of relatives, delivery men, and wayward Sunday drivers. Through some non-verbalized communication sometime prior to our marriage, my wife has been charged with cold-weather activities like making hot chocolate and keeping the fire roaring, and I am in charge of making sure there are a minimum of abandoned vehicles around our house.

Because of my ancestry, I do not take this responsibility lightly. My forefathers, after all, were constantly fending off unwelcome invaders. It's in my genes. If a vehicle is stuck near the house or along our lane, I will do anything I can to drive it away.

When my brother-in-law discovered he could not get back up my driveway this winter, for example, we determined that his front-wheel drive car required more weight forward. It seemed logical (at least to me) that I would drape my considerable frame over the hood and try to stay aboard as he careened to the top. We would have made it on the first try, too, had I not slipped off, and I blame the windshield wipers for that. Windshield wipers made in America should have never broken off like they did.

Men, I have noticed, have a tendency to become more stuck than women. That is because men view becoming stuck as a personal challenge to their masculinity. It's the same reason men don't ask directions. When a woman is spinning her wheels in mud or slushy snow, she will usually stop while the vehicle may still be retrieved. A man, on the other hand, will keep punching the accelerator until he is sideways in the ditch or only the tip of the antenna is showing. During this process, no fewer than a dozen other men will stop and encourage the unfortunate one to "Just rock it." To my knowledge, this technique has not been used successfully since early times when the pioneers tossed stones at their oxen to encourage them to move.

Which all gets me back to the fact that I no longer sigh for winter's end until maybe April. Even then, I take a long, careful look around before I do. And I always keep the snow tires on until May.

From the Desk of Alan Liere

Dear Bert,

I know you were talking about *this* season when you asked me to contact you when the duck hunting got good. Well, I would have, ol' ex-pastor of mine, but it didn't happen—not around here, anyway. I tried calling a couple times, but as I once mentioned when you were tending the flock in these parts, I don't like listening to church music when I'm on hold. Without the choir there to miss the high notes, I feel like I'm in a funeral parlor.

I was really looking forward to busting a few caps with you, and the season was shaping up as a dandy, but we got a terrible ice storm just before Thanksgiving and the waterfowl blew right on through. I hear there was great shooting in the southern part of the state, but around Loon Lake, there were some awfully long faces in December and January. Seems sort of ironic that the best season in two decades produced a total of seven mallards for me—one day's limit. Maybe had I hunted with a man of the cloth, I would have done better, but I couldn't see you driving 350 miles on a "maybe."

I trust you have not regretted the move from Loon Lake to Seattle. When a man moves from the middle to the edge of a major flyway, he's got to have some major motivation. Pansy Widdle wants to know if you'll be back to play shortstop on the softball team this spring, and Racine Delamonte says you forgot to give her your squash casserole recipe before you left. Great to know you're missed, isn't it? Deacon Gruenhagen, your former center fielder and organist, says he will lead the benediction at the wild game dinner this April, and I guess he deserves another chance, but I dread it. Deke has a weakness for Lacey's huckleberry hooch. The last time we asked him to lead the benediction, he blew out the votive candles on the table and started singing "Happy Birthday." Still, it wasn't as embarrassing as the time he struck up the wedding march at Lena Ledbabble's funeral.

I ran into your ex-son-in-law, Morris, at the Dinner Bell Cafe last Saturday morning. He asked me if I'd rolled my pickup. I haven't. But it's funny, isn't it, how if you stick with something long enough, you don't notice the accumulation of rust and dents and squeaks and growls? Lacey says that's why we're still married. We look as good to each other today as we did the day you tied the knot, but boy-oh-boy are our friends changing! Aging is a rather interesting phenomenon, isn't it, Bert? Use to be it depressed me, but now I value the passing years as a means of wearing off the shine. A man, like a good shotgun, isn't worth a damn until the gloss is gone. Next time I see Morris, I'll remember to tell him that.

Our slightly irregular neighbor, Durwood Pickle, is still giving me a hard time about the early goose season they had on the Snake River last September. It seems marina, park, and golf course clientele were growing weary of scraping green goose residue from their shoes, and to accommodate them, the state opened the season for a week in hopes of eliminating or at least scaring off a couple hundred honkers. Long before that, Durwood had decided Canada geese were endangered, having read this erroneous "fact" in a piece of literature he received in the mail from an animal rights organization whose rallying cry was "Birds

Are People, Too!" Any reputable organization, I told him, would not be saying such slanderous things about birds, but Durwood is not about to change any of his mindless opinions—all of which come from pamphlets published by people who think if we had eliminated hunting there would still be 20 million buffalo just outside Des Moines. Durwood is very comfortable with these publications as they provide the security of not having to formulate opinions of his own.

I guess I didn't tell you about my new dog, did I? Her name is Sadie, named after a dubious "lady" in *All the King's Men*, the best book not written by Robert Ruark I've ever read. Sadie is half black Lab and half golden retriever—very much like a golden Lab but with a darker nose and a coat the color of wet wheat stubble. After a slow start, she's really coming on. In fact, until early October, I was feeling pretty smug about paying so little for a decent retriever. That's when I took her with me to build a new blind on that scab rock pond out by Lamont and she got bit in the face by a rattler. What with the anti-venom and the overnight stay at the vet's, she's not such a bargain anymore, but whaddaya gonna do, Bert? Once you're attached, that's all she wrote.

And that's all I wrote, too, Bert. It's your turn. Everyone at Loon Lake (except Durwood) sends their best to the Reverend Bertram Sinn from the Big City On The West Side.

Still your wayward lamb,

Alan

The Most Obliging Critter I Know

Back when I was still trying to decide whether to chase girls or run from them, my grade school had a pet show. As I recall, it was Jimmy Mossy who dazzled the judges and won a blue ribbon with his Nubian goat—not all that unique by rural standards, but pretty darn impressive in suburbia. Davey Williams' dog, Pard, won something, too, but I'm not sure now if it was a red second or a white third. I just remember I was pretty upset Pard won anything at all because earlier that month, he had eaten my hamster, Art.

My fondest memory of that pet show was Arletta Kostelecky and her pet worm. Like myself, Arletta didn't really have an entry when the competition was announced, and I thought it took a lot of brass later for her to pretend she was disappointed her worm didn't win Best of Show. Arletta picked her "Mr. Wiggle" off a wet sidewalk on the way to school the day of the show, but she nevertheless found a pretty little box to display him in, and when other members of our third-grade class were leading their pets around an improvised rink in the gymnasium, Arletta proudly carried hers in outstretched hands. He wouldn't do any tricks, she explained, because he was a tad "strong-willed" and hadn't yet been to obedience school. When Miss Cull, our principal and one of the judges, attempted a closer examination of Arletta's pride, Arletta jerked her hand back and warned Miss Cull to keep her distance. "He's a one-woman worm," she said with a straight face. "He don't take kindly to strangers." I didn't tell anyone at the time, but I thought Mr. Wiggle prettier than Jimmy's goat and a whole lot nicer than Davey or Pard.

When I got home that afternoon, I went digging for a pet or two of my own. In an hour I had collected and named a whole "kennel" full of soft-bodied bilateral invertebrates, but it didn't take many days to discover that soft-bodied bilateral invertebrates were kind of boring, weren't very cuddly, and didn't take well to training. Oh, sometimes they appeared to pick up speed when I called them, but it was never in a consistent direction, and they couldn't speak, heel, or even sit. Shaking hands was out of the question. I think I saw one roll over once, but with a worm, it's hard to tell.

Fortunately for me, I had an Uncle Pat who had artfully avoided full-time employment for over 30 years and who used what he called "down time" to go fishing. It amounted to about six days a week. When I told Uncle Pat about my prodigious accumulation of worms, we became best buddies. Worms, he told me, were about the best fish bait around.

Uncle Pat was right. After that, he began coming by the house for me every Saturday. I would donate my newly-acquired worms and a quarter for gas, and we would drive his rusted, green Buick to whatever lake, pond, stream, or river he had dreamed about the night before. In a day, we would sometimes go through six dozen wigglers and I stopped naming my "pets" because they didn't stay around long enough for me to form an attachment. That, in fact, was one of the things I liked best about worms—they weren't missed much after they were gone. Because of the previous heart-wrenching incident with my hamster and Davey's dog, I was not ready to form a permanent bond with a creature of any genus. With fishing worms, that wasn't a problem.

Today, though I maintain an affection for, I have still not formed one solitary bond with a worm in any of my many bait boxes. This is because I like to catch fish. When angling is tough and I've developed a taste for fillets, nothing beats garden hackle for the freshwater species. Worms are the most obliging critter I know. Worms uncomplicate fishing.

You'd think that when you impale a worm on a size eight hook and toss him overboard, he'd be upset. Instead, he hangs on and wiggles enticingly—exactly what you wanted. Even after a half hour of such abuse, the worm is still down there thumbing his nose at fish, goading them to strike. I have taken as many as eight panfish on a single worm, and once during an ice fishing expedition up north, ran out of bait and still caught fish on a hook bare of anything but worm *smell.*

There are numerous methods for acquiring earthworms, the easiest being to buy them in little Styrofoam containers with plastic lids, but I find digging them myself more satisfying and I wish everyone else did too; I hate seeing Styrofoam and plastic lids littering the banks of my fishing holes. Worms are practically maintenance-free if you keep them in the garden. Like the independent longhorns of old, they prefer an open range, dodging robins and rototillers and generally building stamina and fine character. I have tried on several occasions to capture and raise worms, but they are extremely possessive of their freedom. No matter what precautions I have taken, they are never there in my box or tub when it is time to go fishing. Whether this has been the result of theft, mass suicide, or a well-orchestrated escape, I do not know, but for me it is nevertheless more effective to let them forage for themselves. By digging my own, I can gather fishing bait while pretending my primary motivation is spading the weeds in the flower beds.

I once tried a home-made electric probe for gathering worms, but it wasn't grounded correctly, and my initial venture onto a damp lawn knocked me on my grass and set off a tingling in my fillings that didn't subside for a week. I have a friend who insists he can raise worms to the surface by driving a pitchfork into the ground and smacking the handle vigorously with a 2x4. I tried this once in my yard, however, and right after the lady next door came out and hustled her children into the house, a Sheriff's car pulled up in front. The officer got out and hustled quietly up the driveway. So intent was I in smacking the pitchfork, I didn't see him until he spoke.

"You mad at that pitchfork, mister?" he asked slowly.

At the sound of his voice, I jumped.

"Did that little 'ol pitchfork hurt you?" he continued with a tone somewhere between sympathy and sarcasm.

"Hurt? Why. . . no. . . well. . . .maybe a little. . . .My hands, don'tcha know. Vibrations, I mean. . . I. . . ." I grinned sheepishly. "I'm smacking worms," I explained.

The oficer nodded as if he understood, then moved cautiously closer, keeping his eyes on the 2x4 in my hand. "Don't you think it would be quicker just to stomp the little suckers before they had a chance to crawl up that pitchfork handle?" he asked seriously.

While I am no longer very receptive to worm-procurement methods other than digging, I'm not beyond at least *investigating* something different if it looks interesting. I am currently reading a most fascinating book entitled *Worms Eat My Garbage,* published in 1982 by a lady named Mary Appelhof who insists worms are simple to raise in a system she calls vermicomposting. The book details all sorts of worm lore. I especially liked the chapter on mucous secretions, though there is also some interesting reading about earthworm mating and cocoon formation. In chapter 11, Ms. Appelhof debunks the cherished childhood myth that cutting a worm in two will give you two worms. If cut in the right place, she says, the anterior (head) end of a worm *can* grow a new tail, but the posterior (tail) will never grow a new head. What you usually get are two dead worm parts—still probably enough for half a day of fishing.

Essentially, worms can be classified in two major groups—alive and dead, but unlike minnows or crawdads, they do not have to be particularly lively to catch fish; their mere appearance on a hook is sufficient to trigger a feeding response Even long dead, they provide a stinkbait that is deadly for many species of fish and a sure way to keep prowlers out of the garage. Rather than use a can or worm box, my single friend, Ed, places his worms and a handful of wet moss directly into a front shirt pocket when he goes crick fishing. That way, he tells me, they are not only accessible but impossible to misplace. Should they be forgotten, and the shirt hung in the closet at day's end, his entire wardrobe can be used as a stinkbait the next time he goes fishing. You just can't go wrong with worms.

Cleaning the Creek

Lacey and I spent the last Saturday in March trying to clean out the creek behind the house. Oh, we didn't get too terribly ambitious-nothing that would set off the E.P.A. or alter a salmon migration should salmon ever decide to swim up to Loon Lake, checking out the culverts along Highway 95. No, we just pulled out some of the fallen pine and poisonous nightshade that has been clogging the water since the big fire in '91, hoping that with some clear-running stretches the creek could flush away much of the mud and debris and begin to heal itself.

Besides the obvious gratification to be derived from cleaning up a really big mess, I was anxious to get in the water. Lacey had bought me a new pair of hip waders for our anniversary, and I didn't see any sense in waiting until our summer trip to the Northwest Territory to try them out. There is something about hip waders in cold water that makes me feel extremely smug. Hip waders allow me to go places I'm not supposed to go, and there is a certain exhilaration derived from watching the water creep towards the tops of the boots. With hip waders, I can thumb my nose at the elements-challenge Mother Nature to arm wrestle.

I hadn't been in the water 15 seconds when I noticed my right foot was not staying as warm as my left. A quick inspection revealed this was because I already had a small L-shaped tear near a seam and my right boot was full of water; Mother Nature and a piece of barbed wire had won the first round. My options were to quit right then and know I had wasted the hour I spent gathering tools and getting organized, or to continue with a boot full of frigid water and take the chance of never feeling my toes again. Never a real big fan of toes, I opted to continue.

Less than five minutes later, I eliminated the possible inconvenience of losing the toes on only *one* foot by getting my left foot stuck in the mud and literally walking out of my boot. Now, *both* feet were wet. Two-zip in favor of Mother Nature. To compound my disappointment, l then tripped and sat down in mid-stream. Immediately, I was wet to the waist, and some of my most cherished body parts were quickly going numb.

Stubbornness has always been a Liere family trait, a peculiarity so intense, we even pass it on to our spouses. Not until Lacey and I had cleaned out what we deemed a respectable section of creek did we slosh up the hill to the house. By then, Marie was wet too, and our faces were patterned with splotches of rank creek mud.

It may have been my imagination, but the creek looked a whole lot better Sunday morning from the bedroom window, which, unfortunately was as far as I got, owing to the muscle spasm in my lower back and the fact my neck was so stiff my chin seemed fused to my chest. Cleaning out creeks is evidently not part of my body's job description.

I attempted to get dressed, but couldn't bend over, and to save my soul, I couldn't get my underwear on. Socks were out of the question. I tried draping myself across the bed on my back with my knees pulled up to my chest so I could lasso my toes with the leg-holes of my shorts, but my arms weren't long enough and my aim wasn't true. I tried maneuvering my way to the stairs, thinking I could sit on the landing and the difference in elevation would give me some advantage, but when Lacey came back from the barn where she was giving her chickens a pep *talk,* my big toes were thoroughly entangled in the fabric, my feet were above my head, and I was half way down the staircase, flopping like a piece of tarp caught in the wind.

Unfortunately, our new neighbor, Mrs. Lampwell, was with my wife, and though she tried, it's pretty hard to ignore a nude slapstick routine when all you're expecting is a cup of coffee. Eventually, Lacey got me dressed, but by that time I was so humiliated I just went back to bed. It was doubtful I could have done anything with the day anyway. Mother Nature in a blow-out.

Marty

I met him again at an NRA banquet in town. Same goofy grin, same curly hair. A little heavier than the last time I saw him 30 years ago, but after three decades a few extra pounds, if not an obligation, are certainly an entitlement—like spoiling your grandkids or buying a truck for comfort rather than economy.

Dinner was still a half hour away and I was trying to decide whether I really needed to bid on a little SKB double twenty. Silent auctions were fun, it was for a good cause, and I imagined my wife wouldn't complain too much if I bought a third shotgun. It was already over-priced, though, and Lacey had almost convinced me we needed the carved, over-priced pintail for our mantle. "Hey buddy," he boomed from across the table. "You can't take it with ya!"

I looked up. There was an awkward pause while I tried to make a connection, his crooked, expectant smile prodding me to hurry. "Marty?" I guessed.

His hand reached across the table and I was shaking it. "Long time, buddy," he said. "I hardly recognized you. " He pumped my hand several times, then slowly relaxed his grip. "You still mad at me?" he chuckled.

"Still mad at. . . ?" I'd almost forgotten. The "falling out." The "Great Injustice."

Inseparable through junior high and high school, Marty and I had double-dated to the senior prom, enrolled in the same college, closed down the same bars. Marty was the one who had convinced me to try bird hunting. He was there the day I'd shot my first rooster and the day I'd shot my first drake. Marty had been an usher at my wedding.

Over the ensuing years, though Marty and I had continued to hunt together, there had been times at the end of the day when I felt dirty by association. For some reason, Marty couldn't give up the immature, sometimes irresponsible, bird-in-the-bag mentality of our younger days. Then, he began to surround himself with slight, adoring, unmeritable people who were drawn by his irrepressible personality; I jokingly called them his da-da's. Sometimes he would drag one or more of them along on our excursions afield.

As time went on, our relationship deteriorated further. Eventually, the da-da's weren't funny anymore. Marty and his new friends didn't *flagrantly* violate game laws, but they *did* violate them—shooting at hen pheasants because they couldn't say for sure they weren't roosters, or going over the limit on ducks because "We didn't count so good." One time I stopped to ask permission to hunt at a farm house where three cock pheasants strutted in the driveway. No one was home, and when I got back to the car, Marty and his da-da for the day wanted to shoot the birds from the car window.

The "Falling Out," as my wife called it, came during the second week in September. I'd found a sweet spot near a grain elevator off the Snake River where the doves swarmed over in the evening, racing the sunset on their way to roost in the peach orchards. The shooting lasted mere minutes, but it was furious. Instinctively, I told Marty about it, and three evenings in a row, we'd had the place to ourselves.

Then, on a Friday afternoon, after finishing work early, I decided to head alone to the dove spot. What better way to kick off the weekend? It was an hour's drive, but I would get there in plenty of time.

Marty was there when I arrived. So were a half dozen da-da's. When he saw me, he instinctively crouched down in the weeds, then sensing the futility, strode toward me grinning. "Hey buddy!" he said. "We've got 'em surrounded for you!"

For a moment, my rage made me speechless. Then, it

spewed like molten lava, leveling everything before it. Marty had violated an unspoken trust. This was *my* spot; those were *my* doves! It was not his to give away or even to share. My vicious, verbal barrage cowered them all. Marty was the last to climb sheepishly into the car. "I don't ever want to see you here again!" I screamed. Until the NRA banquet, I hadn't seen him at all.

In retrospect, it had been an accumulation of irritations rather than the one incident, but that had been 30 years ago, and now Marty stood across from me grinning and asking if I was still mad. I didn't think so. Thirty years can heal a lot of sores.

"So how's it goin', Marty?" I asked.

"It's been a ride," he chuckled. "A real ride. Got a house in Florida and a ranch in Wyoming. Shot a six-point bull this year. What a pain! Had to get out of the hot tub to gut it. Flew down to Argentina last year and killed a couple million doves, then. . . ."

I smiled and nodded and didn't say a word. Marty's ride, my dance. Yes, it *had* been a good one, but Marty had ridden one direction, and I had waltzed off in another. "Well, nice seein' you again," I interrupted, turning slowly away. Perhaps I, also, was a slight man for doing so, but sometimes even 30 years isn't nearly long enough.

About the Author

Besides writing a weekly newspaper column for the *Deer Park Tribune*, and a monthly for *The Reel News*, Alan Liere is an award-winning columnist for *Wing and Shot* and *Wildfowl* magazines. Between voluntary skirmishes with his word-processor and hostile engagements with assorted other hateful mechanical devices, he hunts, fishes, and attempts to find a bird dog that will treat him with respect. For 29 years, Mr. Liere has flirted with early senility and bladder failure as an English teacher in the Mead School District. He has two previous collections, *. . . .and pandemonium rained*, published in 1997, and *Bear Heads and Fish Tales* published in 1988.

The Artist

The front and back covers of *Dancin' With Shirley*, were done by Mark Stenersen, a 19-year-old graduate of Spokane's Mead High School. While at Mead, Mark won the Departmental Award in art and the Chad Weaver Memorial Sports Award. He is currently enrolled in the art program at Western Washington University. He hopes to someday apply his considerable talent in creating computer games.

To order additional copies of this book:

Send $14.95 plus $3. postage and handling (U.S.) funds to :
Pease Mountain Publications
P.O. Box 216
Deer Park, WA 99006

SAVE BIG! Order two or more copies at $14.95 each and Pease Mountain Publications assumes shipping and handling fees.

Other Alan Liere titles:
　Bear Heads and Fish Tales
　　　$9.95 plus $2 postage and handling
　. . . .*and pandemonium rained*
　　　$14.95 plus $3 postage and handling

SAVE! Order both of the above for $24.90 post paid.
SAVE AGAIN! Order all three Liere books for $37.50 post paid.
　For personalized, autographed copies, please include name of recipient.